Grow old
along with me

Grow old
along with me

IAN R. K. PAISLEY

AMBASSADOR
Belfast Northern Ireland Greenville South Carolina

Grow Old Along With Me

Copyright © 1999 Ian R. K. Paisley

All rights reserved
No part of this book may be reproduced, stored in a retrieval system, or transmitted in any form or by any means - electronic, mechanical, photocopy, recording or otherwise - without written permission of the publisher, except for brief quotations in printed reviews.

ISBN 1 84030 070 1

Ambassador Publications
a division of
Ambassador Productions Ltd.
Providence House
16 Hillview Avenue,
Belfast, BT5 6JR
Northern Ireland

Emerald House
1 Chick Springs Road, Suite 203
Greenville,
South Carolina 29609, USA
www.emeraldhouse.com

Foreword

THE DAY WE WERE BORN we started to grow old.

The term 'growing old' is mostly used of those who have attained their 60's, 70's, 80's or 90's but the whole process of life is a process of growing old.

The babe is growing old - the child is growing old - the youth is growing old - the mature person is growing old, and the elderly are growing old.

My book is addressed to those in the final category.

Old age should be contemplated. It is a challenge to be faced and an experience not to be endured but enjoyed.

To the believer in the Lord Jesus Christ, growing old in this category is actually the shortening of the distance between them and Heaven, and the approaching of the land of eternal youthfulness.

Our forefathers wrote books about contemplating old age and death, and they were right. The fact of our leaving this world should be constantly contemplated and the last miles of the journey on earth should be under constant preview.

Growing old, approaching heaven, getting closer to saying goodbye to this world should be an experience of real joy and not of grief.

After a journey and long absence from home, as we return and come near to our home again, what anticipation and happiness fill our spirit! If this is true in the natural, how much more in the spiritual.

This book is written so that those of us who are growing old might reap from that experience the last harvest of spiritual joys before entering into the unending joys of our homecoming to the Father's house.
Join me now as we seek to explore this wonderful experience.

IAN R. K. PAISLEY MP, MEP
Belfast
October 1999

List of contents

1 The privilege *of growing old* 9

2 The pangs *of growing old* 15

3 The pleasures *of growing old* 23

4 The perils *of growing old* 33

5 The powerlessness *of growing old* 43

6 The plague *of growing old* 51

7 The potency *of growing old* 61

8 The prospects *of growing old* 73

APPENDIX ONE: *The Four Windows of Life* 95

1 The privilege
of growing old

OLD AGE, IT HAS BEEN SAID, will be bright if we remember that our soul does not age.

It was well said by Sam Weller of Charles Dickens' Mr Pickwick, *"Blest if I don't think his heart was born twenty five years after his body."*

Because Caleb followed the Lord fully he was youthful when he was eighty years of age, *"As yet I am as strong this day as I was in the day that Moses sent me: as my strength was then, even so is my strength now, for war, both to go out, and to come in. Now therefore give me this mountain, whereof the Lord spake in that day; for thou heardest in that day how the Anakims were there, and that the cities were great and fenced: if so be the Lord will be with me then I shall be able to drive them out, as the Lord said. And Joshua blessed him, and gave unto Caleb the son of Jephunneh Hebron for an inheritance. Hebron therefore became the inheritance of Caleb the son of Jephunneh the Kenezite unto this day, because that he wholly followed the Lord God of Israel"* Joshua 14:11-14.

Ageing is a privilege to be enjoyed, not a plague to be endured. You can be youthful in the best possible sense though old.

Growing old is a coronation, not a condemnation.

Listen to this, *"The hoary head is a crown of glory, if it be found in the way of righteousness"* Proverbs 16:31

The silver tongued preacher of Scotland's Victorian era, Dr Thomas Guthrie said, "They say I am growing old because my hair is silvered, and there are crows feet on my forehead, and my step is not as firm and elastic as before.

"But they are mistaken; that is not me. The knees are weak but that is not me. The brow is wrinkled but the brow is not me. This is the house I live in; but I am young, younger than I ever was before."

Sometimes there are those who flit sooner than others. Then there are those and the house has fallen in before they take their leave. There is one thing sure, we will only flit in God's time, not a second before or a second too late.

No wonder another great Scotch Presbyterian preacher, Dr (Rabbi) Duncan, always wished his students at the first of the new year "*A happy eternity*" and not the common "A happy new year".

Dr Guthrie, whom I have already mentioned, narrates the following in his life story, a part of his autobiography I have never forgotten after more than forty years since first reading it.

"The case of Dr Alison, the celebrated physician, and hardly less famous philanthropist, one of the best and greatest men I ever knew, was much more extraordinary. It recalls the days of the patriarchs. He, dying in 1859, had spoken to a man who had spoken to a man who had been at Flodden Field, a battle fought as far back as 1513. There was, so to speak, but one man between him and an event that occurred more than three hundred years before. What seems incredible is thus explained: - when a mere child, Dr Alison had been put in the arms of a man in Aberdeenshire, who lived, if I remember aright, to the age of a hundred and thirty; and this old highland patriarch had once met with Jenkins - who survived till he was a hundred and sixty-nine years old, and had when a boy carried arrows to the English archers who fought and won the field at Flodden.

"One of the most curious cases of old age I ever heard of was told me by Lord Ardmillan, who, to the integrity of a judge, and the graces of a genius, and the piety of a Christian, adds such a knack for story telling as makes his society quite delightful. Mr F Dundas MP, a friend of his, having heard when on a visit to Shetland, of a very old man who lived on the mainland, or one of its islands, went to see him. On approaching his cottage, he saw an aged but hale-looking man at work in a field close by, and not doubting but that this was the person he was in search of, he made up to him, but had no sooner begun to moralise on topics suitable to old age and the close of life, than the person he addressed turned round on him to say, "It'll be my fayther ye've come to see; there he is, sitting at the cheek o' the door!" And there, on walking up to the house, he saw a grey-haired, venerable patriarch, sitting on a stone by the door, warming his cold blood in the sunshine. On going up to him, and introducing himself as a traveller, who had come out of his way to see one who had seen so many years, he was much surprised when this old man, pointing his staff to the door, said, "It'll be my fayther ye've come to see; he's in the house, there!" He entered: and there, in one who, with bleared eyes and furrowed brow, cowered over a peat fire, while he stretched out his palsied hands to catch its warmth, and over whose shoulders, bent under the weight of years, fell a few spare silver locks, he saw the very picture of a great old age. He was sure that he had now got hold of the veritable man. Raising his voice, for he found the aged patriarch deaf almost as a door-post, he let him know the purpose of his visit. But what was his astonishment when this withered form by the "chimney neuk," pointing to the door of an inner room, said, "Oh, it'll be my fayther ye've come to see; he's ben there!" and an old woman who sat by the fire, added, "Surely, sir, you'll not go till you've seen 'the Lucky Dad'?" And "ben there," to be sure, lying in a "box-bed" he found the father of the other three generations, alive indeed, but more like a dried mummy than a living man."

It may not be desirable to live on into second childhood - man, in such a condition, presenting physically and mentally, as well as morally and spiritually, the saddest of all ruins. Yet the glory of God and the good of mankind require that we do ourselves no harm, but, devoting it to useful, noble, and holy purposes spin out our life till the thread snaps through sheer tenuity and weakness.

If we grow old however, in the way of grace we can also grow old gracefully and be rich.

Rich in experience that angels might covet,
Rich in faith that has grown with age.

Those who are ageing have a job of work to do and should be spurred into activity by the Scripture exhortation *"the night cometh when no man can work"*.

I am reminded of Longfellow's great poem:

Tell me not, in mournful numbers,
Life is but an empty dream!
For the soul is dead that slumbers,
And things are not what they do seem.

Life is real! and life is earnest!
And the grave is not its goal;
Dust thou art, to dust returnest,
Was not spoken of the soul.

Not enjoyment, and not sorrow
Is our destined end or way;
But to act, that each tomorrow
Find us further than today.

Art is long, and time is fleeting,
And our hearts, though stout and brave,
Still, like muffled drums, are beating
Funeral marches to the grave.

In the world's broad field of battle,
Is the bivouac of life,
Be not like dumb, driven cattle!
Be a hero in the strife!

Trust no future, howe'er pleasant!
Let the dead past bury its dead!
Act - act in the living present!
Heart within, and God o'erhead!

Lives of great men all remind us
We can make our lives sublime,
And, departing, leave behind us
Footprints on the sand of time -

Footprints that perhaps another,
Sailing o'er life's solemn main,
A forlorn and shipwrecked brother,
Seeing, shall take heart again.

Let us, then, be up and doing,
With a heart for any fate;
Still achieving, still pursuing,
Learn to labour and to wait.

Some time ago I read the following lines. They are most appropriate.

I love aged mothers - mothers with white hair,
And kindly eyes, and lips grown softly sweet
With murmured blessings over sleeping babes.
There is something in their quiet grace
That speaks the calm of Sabbath afternoons;
A knowledge in their deep unfaltering eyes
That far outreaches all philosophy.

Time, with caressing touch, about them weaves
The silver-threaded fairy-shawl of age;
While all the echoes of forgotten songs
Seem joined to lend a sweetness to their speech.

Old mothers! As they pass, with slow-timed step,
Their trembling hand clings gently to youth's strength.
Sweet mothers! As they pass, one sees again
Old garden walks, old roses, and old loves.

When the late Dr James MacGregor of Edinburgh reached his 39th birthday, 11th July, 1868, he said, "I am a good way past the summit level of life. Road henceforth all downhill. I give thanks to God that He has spared my life so long, and ask His forgiveness for its manifold sins and shortcomings, and pray Him for grace to give my future time unreservedly to him." When George Watts, the great painter, was just twice that age, he wrote to a friend: "I think I am quite accurate in telling you that I saw the sun rise every day last summer. I am 78 now, and I have still to do my best work.

"O God, thou hast taught me from my youth: and hitherto have I declared thy wondrous works. Now also when I am old and grayheaded, O God, forsake me not; until I have shewed thy strength unto this generation and thy power to every one that is to come." Psalm 71:17-18.

Yes, youth is not it all. It is but part of the whole and the end should be better. Let me close with the lines.

Grow old along with me,
The best is yet to be -
The last of life, for which
The first was made.

2 The pangs *of growing old*

IN THE LAST CHAPTER I spoke of the privilege of growing old. Some have never appreciated the privilege or counted its many blessings.

Alas, they are more and more obsessed with the pangs of growing old.

THE PANGS OF PHYSICAL WEAR

The body, that mechanism so fearfully and wonderfully made, as it ages, will have its pangs. You can expect them. You should prepare for them. You should be able to handle them when they come.

'Tis a mortal body we inhabit on earth. It is an earthly house of this tabernacle which we tenant. In parts of Northern Ireland the houses were built of earth. It was quite a feat to construct them and many of them lasted well. They were so well white-washed that until closer examination it was difficult to discover that they were dried out mud houses.

But all human bodies are of this earth, earthy. Of the dust they are all made and to the dust they shall return.

We ought to expect that the marks of wear and tear must sooner or later show themselves upon them. They are but mortal bodies at the very best.

The moment we commenced living we commenced dying. The entrance to this life leads directly, and how swiftly, to the exit.

Without due care and close attention anything will show and manifest signs of decay, declension and distress.

Why, this whole earth groans, with its weight of years and troubles, through and through with expectancy *"The whole creation groaneth and travaileth together until now - waiting"* Romans 8:22-23

The storms of life are bound to leave their marks upon our frames. The burden and heat of many days leaves us not unpoxed. The hard road, the bitter winds, the rough sojournings, the uphill path and the water of river floods and seas all take their toll upon our bodies.

If it were not so it surely would be passing strange.

I used to hear, when I was a boy in Ballymena, the expression about an elderly person who kept their freshness, *"They're well preserved!"* Yes, preserved indeed, for their bodies had to take the pressures of life like everyone else. Preserved or not, the body hastens on to its dissolution.

When we feel our aches and pains let us remember the times when we had no such symptoms. Let us thank God for what our eyes did see, though now they are dimmed, what our ears did hear, though now they are deaf, what our hands did hold, though now they are weak, what our arms did embrace, though now they are feeble, what paths our feet did traverse, though now they are foot sore and weary, what places our legs did carry us, though now they are no longer strong. Thanksgiving to God and praises to our Saviour are healing medicine for the bodily pangs of growing old.

Yes, and when the death pangs come and the body lies still in death, and the skin worms destroy, never forget its past nor its future.

> Behold this ruin! 'Twas a skull
> Once of ethereal spirit full.
> This narrow cell was Life's retreat,
> This space was Thought's mysterious seat.
> What beauteous visions filled this spot?
> What dreams of pleasure, long forgot?
> Nor hope, nor joy, nor love, nor fear,
> Have left one trace of record here.

Beneath this mouldering canopy
Once shone the bright and busy eye,
But start not at the dismal void -
If social love that eye employed,
If with no lawless fire it gleamed,
But through the dews of kindness beamed,
That eye shall be forever bright
When stars and sun are sunk in night.

Within this hollow cavern hung
The ready, swift, and tuneful tongue;
If Falsehood's honey it disdained,
And when it could not praise was chained;
If bold in Virtue's cause it spoke,
Yet gentle concord never broke -
This silent tongue shall plead for thee
When Time unveils Eternity!

Say, did these fingers delve the vein?
Or with the envied rubies shine?
To hew the rock or wear a gem
Can little now avail to them.
But if the page of Truth they sought,
Or comfort to the mourner brought,
These hands a richer meed shall claim
Than all that wait on Wealth and Fame.

Avails it whether bare or shod
These feet the paths of duty trod?
If from the bowers of Ease they fled,
To seek Affliction's humble shed;
If Grandeur's guilty bride they spurned,
And home to Virtue's cot returned -
These feet with angel-wings shall vie,
And tread the palace of the sky!

Let us bless God for every bodily pang of the past, present and future in the sure and certain hope that these very pangs will give place to everlasting praises.

THE PANGS OF MENTAL SCARES

What tricks our mind, when under stress, can play on us! What scares they give us.

Yes, as we grow old the pangs of deep regrets at times darken our vision and rob us of the enjoyment of God's peace which passeth knowledge and all understanding. A stirred up memory with its unceasing waves of regrets creates mental scares.

The evil things of memory drown the good, and the damnable sins of youth are resurrected to haunt and torment our spirits.

Let us always remember that it matters not what our memories may cast up, and what suggestions the Tempter may parade, all our sins and all our guilty past are obliterated from the memory of God.

Oh what peace is this! Oh what joy is this!

Oh what solace is this!

"I, even I, am He that blotteth out thy transgressions for mine own sake and will not remember thy sins."

No wonder the young Covenanter, Margaret Wilson, as the Solway Firth's swollen tide rolled in to take away her life and send her to heaven for a martyr's crown, sang with joyous voice -

"My sins and faults of youth
Do Thou O Lord forget:
After Thy mercy think on me
And for Thy goodness great. (Psalm 25:7)

The blood of Jesus Christ not only purges our sins from our heart forever but erases their memory from the memory of God forever.

THEY ARE ALL GONE FOREVER

I came across these lines the other day, they are well worth pondering. They ask a most pertinent question:

Which Road?

If you could go back to the fork of the road,
Back the long miles you have carried this load,
Back to the place where you had to decide
By this way or that through your life to abide,
Back of the sorrow and back of the care,
Back to the place where the future was fair, -
If you were there now, a decision to make,
O pilgrim of sorrow, which road would you take?

Then, after you'd trodden the other long track.
Suppose that again to the fork you went back,
After you found that its promises fair
Were but a delusion that led to a snare;
That the road you first travelled with sighs and unrest,
Though dreary and rough was most graciously blessed
With balm for each bruise and a charm for each ache, -
O pilgrim of sorrow, which road would you take?

You can rest assured you are on the right road if you have Christ, the Way, the Truth and the Life, in your heart.

THE PANGS OF SPIRITUAL CARE

In growing old there comes oftentimes the pangs of spiritual care.

How Satan would like to drown us in the sea of isolation from our Beloved Saviour and weigh us down with an ever-increasing load of care.

He would accuse us and abuse us with every dart his Satanic fury can muster.

Dark thoughts which make us shudder, flash through our mind and soul.

We torment ourselves needlessly with thoughts about our personal salvation and if we have committed the unpardonable sin. This is an old ploy of the old serpent. How he has used it to the very end to lash the backs of the saints of God.

I remember passing through a period of such dark spiritual oppression and depression. I ought to have shared it with a fellow believer but I did not. Then I heard an old revival preacher from the 1904 Welsh Awakening relate his similar experience. The chains were broken and my soul was freed. I am glad I passed this way for I have been able to help scores of believers in similar temptations. Only the other day I was able to point a young lady, evilly set upon by the devil in this way, to glorious victory. She left God's house rejoicing.

Satan fights hardest at the end of the believer's life for he knows that soon the believer will be right beyond his reach. He has a final Satanic fling at us. As you grow old prepare for this. Clothe yourself in the whole armour of God; seek ever the shelter of the precious blood and plead ever the all-precious, all-powerful overcoming Name of our Lord Jesus.

> Christ's name destroys the Devil's works,
> Beats back the powers of hell.
> And Satan trembles at the name
> Of Him in whom we dwell.

> "Lord, at Thy feet my prostrate heart is lying,
> Worn with the burden, weary of the way;
> The world's proud sunshine on the hills is dying,
> And morning's promise fades with parting day.
> Yet, in Thy light, another morn is breaking,
> Of fairer promise and with pledge more true;
> And in Thy life a dawn of youth is waking,
> Whose bounding pulses shall this heart renew.

> "Oh, to go back across the years long vanished,
> To have the words unsaid, the deeds undone,
> The errors cancelled, the deep shadows banished,
> In the glad sense of a new life begun.

To be a little child, whose page of story
Is yet undimmed, unblotted by a stain,
And in the sunrise of primeval glory
To know that life has had it start again.

"I may go back across the years long vanished,
I may resume my childhood, Lord, in Thee,
When in the shadow of Thy cross are banished
All other shadows that encompass me:
And o'er the road that now is rough and dreary,
Thy soul, made buoyant by a strength divine,
Shall walk untired, shall run and not be weary,
To bear the blessings that have made Thee mine."

3 The pleasures *of growing old*

IN OUR LAST CHAPTER we dwelt upon the pangs of growing old, now we turn to the delightful topic - the pleasures of growing old.

Growing old can be an experience of the most wonderful pleasures when we anchor our soul to the Three Great Impregnables - God's Promise - God's Presence - God's Person.

I. GROW OLD RECOGNISING GOD'S PROMISE

Hear the good Word of the Lord. *"For which cause we faint not; but though our outward man perish yet the inward man is renewed day by day"* II Corinthians 4:16.

What a practical and pleasure creating promise from our faithful God!

Yes, as we grow old we shall experience the wear and tear of our bodies. The body is bound to age. It is a perishing commodity and perishing it will and perish it must. It is dust in its origination and dust is its destination. *"For dust thou art and unto dust thou shalt return"* Genesis 3:19. That was true of Old Man Adam and true of all his sons and daughters as well. When the dust of death comes, to the dust our bodies will go.

But as our bodies are ageing for the process of the return to the dust our inward man, the real person, the immortal being, the redeemed soul, is renewed day by day.

Did you enjoy the pleasure of that renewing today? Oh and what a renewing that is. I sing every morning the 23rd Psalm and what a lift I get from the words experimentally received, *My soul He doth restore again.*

This constant, continual and sustained restoral is the renewing of the inward man.

The outward man is ageing in the sense of feeling the weight of its years. The body is scarred and marred by human infirmities and weaknesses. But the inward man may carry the same number of years but not the same weight of years, for the inward man is growing stronger and stronger while the outward man decayeth.

This is the birthright of the child of God. As your days so shall your strength be. Reckon on this great promise of God. By faith appropriate it. Let it give to you pleasures of which the world and a weak ageing body cannot rob you.

Note its opening words *"For this cause we FAINT NOT"*. Why are you fainting in weakness when you should be demonstrating feats of endurance? Oh feel today the unstoppable life giving surge of power in your inward man and let its accompanying pleasure be a blessed elixir to your entire being. Be 70 or 80 or 90 years young.

When you lose the pleasure you will lose your life itself. You don't lose the thrill because you are old, you are old because you have lost it.

The renewal of the Holy Spirit is His daily repair and maintenance job upon our whole person. Call Him in today., His name is Comforter - One called alongside to help.

Professor Rainy of the Free Church of Scotland fame wrote this to a friend when he completed his eightieth year.

"I hear indeed, that you do not get any younger. Strange to say that is my experience too. But we have a humble hope that the best kind of youth awaits us in another country. The Lord grant it in His wonderful mercy." Even if you are eighty it has been said you haven't lived one day.

Three-score and ten by common calculation
The years of man amount to, but we'll say
He turns four-score, yet in my estimation
In all these years he has not lived a day.

Out of the eighty, you must first remember
The hours of night you pass asleep in bed,
And counting from December to December
Just half your life you'll find you have been dead.

To 40 years at once by this reduction
We come. But during 5 years from your birth,
While cutting teeth and living upon suction,
You're not alive to what your life is worth.

From 35 take for education
15, at least, at college and at school,
When, notwithstanding all your application,
The chances are you may turn out a fool.

Still 20 you have left us to dispose of;
But during them your fortune you've to make,
And granting with the luck of some one knows of
'Tis made in 10, that 10 from life to take.

Out of the 10 yet left you must allow for
The time for shaving, tooth and other aches,
Say 4, that leaves 6 - too short, I vow, for
Regretting past, and making fresh, mistakes

Meanwhile each hour dispels some fond illusion
Until at length sans eyes, sans teeth, you may
Have scarcely sense to come to this conclusion -
You've reached four-score, and haven't lived ONE DAY!

The rhyme may be full of logical fallacies but it makes a vital point.

II. GROW OLD REVELLING IN GOD'S PRESENCE

Ponder these two texts continually, aged believer. They will bring pleasure to your body, soul and spirit.

"My presence shall go with thee and I will give thee rest" Exodus 33:14

"Thou wilt shew me the path of life; in Thy presence is fulness of joy; at Thy right hand there are pleasures for evermore" Psalm 16:11

The place we should live is the sweet presence of the Saviour. Here is the place of eternal youthfulness where our immortal souls can never grow old.

This is the place of the shadow of the wings of Almighty God.

Remember what Boaz said to Ruth, *"The Lord recompense thy work, and a full reward be given thee of the Lord God of Israel, under whose wings thou art come to trust"* Ruth 2:12.

> In the shadow of His wings
> There is rest, sweet rest;
> There is rest from care and labour,
> There is rest for friend and neighbour:
> In the shadow of His wings
> There is rest, sweet rest;
> In the shadow of His wings
> There is rest ...
>
> There is rest! sweet rest!
> There is peace! sweet peace!
> There is joy, glad joy,
> In the shadow of His wings! ¬
>
> In the shadow of His wings
> There is peace, sweet peace:
> Peace that passeth understanding,
> Peace, sweet peace, that knows no ending;

In the shadow of His wings
There is peace, sweet peace,
In the shadow of His wings
There is peace …

In the shadow of His wings
There is joy, glad joy:
There is joy to tell the story,
Joy exceeding, full of glory;
In the shadow of His wings
There is joy, glad joy,
In the shadow of His wings
There is joy

To live in God's presence is to predate heaven, the place of everlasting youthfulness. The ancient angels created before Adam are described in the gospel as being like young men (Mark 16:5).

How sweet our evening years will be with the pleasures of eternity rising up within us and giving us a foretaste of the glory that is to come. Let us practice living in the enjoyment of the rich presence of our loving Saviour, then we will never have the growing old despondency. Never grow old? You can never grow old in the presence of your glorious Lord. He has a special love for you, dear ageing child of God. To Him the grey head is *beauty* (Proverbs 20:29) and the head in the way of righteousness a crown of *glory* (Proverbs 16:31). The more we bask the more we will enjoy the pleasures of growing old.

In the secret of His presence
How my soul delights to hide!
Oh, how precious are the lessons
Which I learn at Jesus' side!
Earthly cares can never vex me,
Neither trials lay me low;
For when Satan comes to tempt me
To the secret place I go.

When my soul is faint and thirsty.
'Neath the shadow of His wing
There is cool and pleasant shelter,
And a fresh and crystal spring;
And my Saviour rests beside me,
As we hold communion sweet;
If I tried, I could not utter,
What He says when thus we meet.

Only this I know: I tell Him
All my doubts and griefs and fears;
Oh, how patiently He listens!
And my drooping soul He cheers.
Do you think He ne'er reproves me?
What a false friend He would be,
If He never, never told me
Of the sins which He must see!

Would you like to know the sweetness
Of the secret of the Lord?
Go and hide beneath His shadow,
This shall then be your reward;
And whene'er you leave the silence
Of that happy meeting place,
You will bear the shining image
Of the Master in your face.
                    - Ellen Lakshmi Goreh

III. GROW OLD REJOICING IN GOD'S PERSON

"Although the fig tree shall not blossom, neither shall fruit be in the vines; the labour of the olive shall fail, and the field shall yield no meat; the flock shall be cut off from the fold, and there shall be no herd in the stalls: Yet I will rejoice in the Lord, I will joy in the God of my salvation." Habakkuk 3:17-18

Any other basis for joy will decay and crumble. There is only one everlasting foundation of satisfying and enduring rejoicing and that is God Himself, the Eternal Three in One and the Eternal One in Three.

Everything else will fail but God cannot fail.
Everything else will weary but God cannot be weary.
Everything else will depart but God cannot depart.
Everything else will change but God cannot change.
Everything else will pass away but God remaineth, He cannot pass away.

Notice how the old revival prophet (see chapters 2 and 3) emphasises the basis of abiding joy.

Habakkuk was a rural dweller. He had grown up with the joys which come from the pastoral and fruit keeper's life, the joys of the plucking of the fruits from the well-tended fig trees and vine trees. How the husbandman rejoices with satisfying pleasure and joy when he handles the fruit of his ardent labours. The winter days, the spring days, the summer days all witnessed his labours, and now the harvest time comes.

But in this instance all the past labours were in vain. The fig tree refused to blossom and the vine refused to bear fruit. No meat of any kind came forth in harvest time from the ploughed and sown fields. A disease smote the flocks, both sheep and goats. The herd in the stalls fell also before the plague. The scene which should have been one of harvest joy was one of total fruitlessness. An awful disease had caused all things to be totally blighted. The outlook was very bleak and very dark.

Habakkuk, however, did not concentrate on the

OUTLOOK BUT ON THE UPLOOK

His vision was far above the blight of the fig trees, the blasting of the vines, the blackness of the fields, the blemish of the folds and the bitterness of the stalls.

His vision was still upward as it passed the birds of the first heaven, the stars of the second heaven and the angels of the third heaven.

It came to a stop only at the throne of the Everlasting God and found the foundation for joy unspeakable in Him who sits on that throne. There in heavenly places it rejoiced in Jehovah and joyed in the God of salvation.

There, far above all principality and power and might and dominion and every name that is hailed, not only in this world but also in that which is to come, it sang its paraphrase of joy and shouted its psalm of rejoicing.

Age loses its weariness here and growing old becomes growing young again.

Do you remember what Caleb said when he was 85? - Joshua 14:7-11. "Forty years old was I when Moses the servant of the Lord sent me to spy out the land ... And now, behold, the Lord hath kept me alive, as He said, these forty and five years ... and now, lo, I am this day fourscore and five years old. As yet I am as strong this day as I was in the day that Moses sent me: as my strength was then, even so is my strength now, for war, both to go out, and to come in." We are not to look on these words as the silly talk of a boastful old man, but as a wonderful proof to us that if our lives are shortened or our welfare hindered by the sin of others, or by unexpected and unusual duty laid on us - and that is a thing that happens to more than we would think - God in His power and love, and in His own way, can restore, and will restore, these lost years to us.

What rejoicing we have when our anchor is held fast in the Eternal Rock of Ages (See Authorised Version margin Isaiah 26:4). This is joy unspeakable and full of glory.

Charles Hodge, described as "the greatest theologian America ever produced" and "the greatest representative of conservative Calvinism in America's last 200 years", aged 76 years, opened the Sixth General Conference of the Evangelical Alliance in New York. In a voice softened with age he prayed:

"Come, Holy Spirit, come! Descend in all Thy plenitude of grace. Come as the Spirit of reverence and love. Aid us, O God, in the discharge of the duties on which we are about to enter. We have assembled here from almost all parts of the world. We have come to confess Thee before men; to avow our faith that God is, and that he is the Creator, Preserver, and Governor of the World. We are here to acknowledge that the God of

Abraham and Isaac, and of Jacob is our God. We are here to confess Christ as God manifest in the flesh, and as our only and all-sufficient Saviour, who for us sinners died upon the cross, to reconcile us unto God, and to make expiation for the sins of men; and who, having died for our offences, has risen again for our justification. We acknowledge Him as now seated at the right hand of the Majesty on high, all power in heaven and on earth having been committed to His hands. Thanks be to God, thanks be to God, that He has put on us, unworthy as we are, the honour to make this confession, and to bear this testimony to God and to His Son. O God, look down from heaven upon us. Shed abroad in our hearts the Holy Spirit, that we may be truly one in Christ Jesus."

"O Thou blessed Spirit of the living God, without whom the universe were dead, Thou art the source of all life, of all holiness, of all power. O Thou perfect Spirit, Thou precious gift of God, come, we pray, and dwell in every heart, and touch every lip. We invoke the blessing of Father, Son and Holy Ghost on this Evangelical Alliance. We spread abroad our banner, in the sight of all men, with the confession which Thou has put on our lips - the confession of all Christendom. We confess God the Father to be our Father; Jesus Christ His Son, to be our Saviour; and the Holy Ghost to be our Sanctifier; and His Word to be the infallible rule of faith and practice. Grant, O Lord, that whatever human words are uttered, this confession may be the language of every heart. And to the Father, Son and Holy Ghost be glory, now and evermore. Amen."

Such a prayer shows that Charles Hodge, though weak and weary in body, in old age was rejoicing in God's Person. He had learned the pleasures of old age.

Hodge's secret - may we all make it ours - is best expressed in the following lines written by Mr Midlane, the author of the hymn *There's A Friend For Little Children*:-

> Life's calm has sweetly come,
> Its waves no longer roar,
> Its eye is on the nearing home,
> Upon the restful shore.

'Twere better youth were age
Than age were youth again;
Youth is regardless of the page
Which age would fear to stain.

Grace, now the better known,
Holds constant watch within,
Hears well each whisper from the throne
To guard the soul from sin.

'Tis contemplation calm,
'Tis radiant forecast given,
Life's closing, tranquil, happy psalm,
The vestibule of heaven.

Herein lie the Pleasures of Old Age.

4 The perils
of growing old

CHILDHOOD HAS ITS PERILS. Youth has its perils. Maturity has its perils and so has old age. But when we come to old age, all our experience cannot deliver us from its peril. Only the grace of God can do that, and the grace of God alone.

The Bible condemns all sins and condones no sin, therefore in its faithful account of the lives of long-lived saints it fearlessly exposes their sin in old age.

Old man **Noah** walked with God when the whole world was out of step with God. He built an ark to the saving of his soul and his family's souls. He became heir of the righteousness which is by faith, yet he fell a prey to the perils of old age.

What a sight is this! Old man Noah lying drunk and naked in his tent and abused by his youngest son!

He lost the very grace which marked his whole life - purity. (See Genesis 6:9 and Genesis 9:20-21.)

Let us all beware and tremble

Abraham fell to the perils of old age and for thirteen years God did not appear unto him, from the age of 86 until the age of 99. *"And Abram was fourscore and six years old, when Hagar bare Ishmael to Abram"* Genesis 16:16.

"And when Abram was ninety years old and nine, the Lord appeared to Abram, and said unto him, I am the Almighty God; walk before me, and be thou perfect. And I will make my covenant between me and thee, and will multiply thee exceedingly. And Abram fell on his face: and God talked with him," Genesis 17:1-3.

No wonder he had to fall flat on his face in penitence when God appeared to him after 13 years. Thirteen in Scripture is the number of apostasy. (First mention Genesis 14:47.)

In the meantime, after obeying Sarah his wife in taking the quick way to get a son and heir, he stooped to lying and deception. Look at Abraham, the father of the faithful, the great man of faith, fallen a prey to the perils of old age.

Let him that thinketh he standeth take heed lest he fall

And look at **Jacob**. He fell a prey to the indulgence of the child of his old age and because of that over-indulgence, fell an easy prey to the deception of his murderous sons.

In his blindness he never asked the all-too-glaring question, *"If Joseph was devoured why was his coat intact?"*

Having fallen a prey to the perils of old age, he became a miserable old man and lost all hope that Joseph, the man of vision, would still see the fulfilment of his dreams. Look at him, so fuelled with unbelief that when he heard Joseph was alive he fainted. What a sad picture of the man of the name-change to "PREVAILING PRINCE WITH GOD".

Beware lest ye also fall into the same condemnation.

And what of his father **Isaac**, thinking he was going to die years before the event? Instead of preparing for death by prayers and communion with God, at which he excelled in his youth (see Genesis 24:63) he indulged his flesh and became an easy prey to Rebecca's and Jacob's deception.

Poor blinded Isaac, giving into his fleshly appetites instead of living in the presence of His God.

Take care lest you too are snared by this devil's bait.

And what of **Moses**?

He excelled in meekness, yet in old age he lost his temper. His anger broke the beautiful type of Christ the Rock smitten only once for our redemption and by striking it twice fortified his right to enter into the promised land.

God's judgment was not reversed and God warned Moses thus.

In the peril of old age he destroyed a life of patience and meekness. Look at him, the Prophet whom our Lord was to be like, in a blind rage!

What a tragedy! If it could happen to the great man Moses how much more easily it could happen to you or me.

And what of **Aaron** the elder brother of Moses?

He was the man who stood between the people and the plague and saved the nation (Numbers 16:48). He was the first High Priest of Israel, the extremely eloquent spokesman for his brother Moses who was slow of speech.

He too, however, fell a prey to the perils of old age.

With Moses he broke the precious type of the once-for-all one striking of Christ at the Cross, and lost his right to enter the Promised Land.

Upon the Mount Hor he was stripped of his garments and they and his forfeited office were given to another.

God's sentence was plain. *"Aaron shall be gathered unto his people; for he shall not enter into the land which I have given unto the children of Israel, because ye rebelled against my word at the water of Meribah"* Numbers 20:24.

What a scene, the first High Priest stripped naked and publicly prepared for the sentence of death passed on him.

Who can escape, if this happened to such an exalted person, the first person to pass the veil and approach the mercy seat of God?

What of **Gideon,** one of the great heroes of faith?

His first great act was to pull down Baal's idolatrous altar at Ophrah, but in later years he substituted it with another idolatrous symbol. *"And Gideon made an ephod thereof, and put it in his city, even in Ophrah: and all Israel went thither a whoring after it: which thing became a snare unto Gideon, and to his house"* Judges 8:27.

Consider Gideon, the champion of God's cause, fallen in old age to erecting a shrine of idolatry where he first laid low the idolatry of Baal.

If Gideon thus fell, ought not we to tremble at the perils of old age?

Then what about another high priest of God, **Eli**? He judged the people of God 40 years but alas did not judge himself.

The faithful record tells us *"Now the sons of Eli were sons of Belial; they knew not the Lord."* I Samuel 2:12 *"And the Lord said to Samuel, Behold, I will do a thing in Israel, at which both the ears of every one that heareth it shall tingle. In that day I will perform against Eli all things which I have spoken concerning his house: when I begin, I will also make an end. For I have told him that I will judge his house for ever for the iniquity which he knoweth; because his sons made themselves vile, and he restrained them not. And therefore I have sworn unto the house of Eli, that the iniquity of Eli's house shall not be purged with sacrifice nor offering for ever"* I Samuel 3:11-14

Eli succumbed to the perils of old age. What an obituary notice the Holy Ghost wrote of him! *"And it came to pass, when he made mention of the ark of God, that he fell from off the seat backward by the side of the gate, and his neck brake, and he died: for he was an old man, and heavy. And he had judged Israel forty years"* I Samuel 4:18.

May God in grace deliver us from such an end, overcome by the perils of old age!

Aye, and what of young **Samuel**? He was God's minister of judgment to Eli (See I Samuel 3:11-14).

When he was old - like Eli - his sons walked not in his ways *"And it came to pass, when Samuel was old, that he made his sons judges over Israel. Now the name of his firstborn was Joel; and the name of his second, Abiah: they were judges in Beer-sheba. And his sons walked not in his ways, but turned aside after lucre, and took bribes, and perverted judgment."* I Samuel 8:1-3.

Poor man, he fell in old age into the very peril which tripped up Eli.

What a sad sight, the holy Samuel being told by the people *"Behold thou art old and thy sons walk not in thy ways: now make us a king to judge us like all the nations"* I Samuel 8:5

Let us learn that there is no discharge ever in the constant war against sin, and especially when we face the perils of old age.

Then we come to **David** the king. What was the Lord's testimony about him in his youth *"a man after his (God's) own heart"* I Samuel 13:14.

What of the ending of his days? In old age he fell a prey to the perils which beset him. He decided to number the people of his kingdom, *"And*

Satan stood up against Israel and provoked David to number Israel" I Chronicles 21:1

Wrath from God fell upon the nation for the king's sin. Listen to his pathetic cry *"And David said unto God, Is it not I that commanded the people to be numbered? even I it is that have sinned and done evil indeed; but as for these sheep, what have they done? let thine hand, I pray thee, O Lord my God, be on me and on my father's house; but not on thy people, that they should be plagued."* I Chronicles 21:17.

What a topple David took in old age! He that thinketh he standeth BEWARE.

Then comes **Solomon,** the beloved of the Lord.

Listen to those words *"In Gibeon the Lord appeared to Solomon in a dream by night: and God said, Ask what I shall give thee. And Solomon said, Thou hast shewed unto thy servant David my father great mercy, according as he walked before thee in truth, and in righteousness, and in uprightness of heart with thee; and thou hast kept for him this great kindness, that thou hast given him a son to sit on his throne, as it is this day. And now, O Lord my God, thou hast made thy servant king instead of David my father: and I am but a little child: I know not how to go out or come in. And thy servant is in the midst of thy people which thou hast chosen, a great people, that cannot be numbered nor counted for multitude. Give therefore thy servant an understanding heart to judge thy people, that I may discern between good and bad: for who is able to judge this thy so great a people? And the speech pleased the Lord, that Solomon had asked this thing. And God said unto him, Because thy hast asked this thing, and hast not asked for thyself long life; neither hast asked riches for thyself, nor hast asked the life of thine enemies; but hast asked for thyself understanding to discern judgment; Behold, I have done according to thy words: lo, I have given thee a wise and an understanding heart; so that there was none like thee before thee, neither after thee shall any arise like unto thee. And I have also given thee that which thou hast not asked, both riches, and honour: so that there shall not be any among the kings like unto thee all thy days. And if thou wilt walk in my ways, to keep my statutes and my commandments, as thy father David did walk, then I will lengthen thy days."* I Kings 3:5-14. And so says the chronicle, "Solomon was king over all Israel."

His greatest work was the building of the temple, and what a temple it was! Made according to the pattern which God gave to David *"Then*

David gave to Solomon his son the pattern of the porch, and of the houses thereof, and of the treasuries thereof, and of the upper chambers thereof, and of the inner parlours thereof, and of the place of the mercy seat, And the pattern of all that he had by the Spirit, of the courts of the house of the Lord, and of all the chambers round about, of the treasuries of the house of God, and of the treasuries of the dedicated things: ... All this, said David, the Lord made me understand in writing by his hand upon me, even all the works of this pattern." I Chronicles 28: 11, 12 and 19.

However, although Solomon was the wisest of all men he fell a prey to the perils of old age.

What a sad record is this! *"For it came to pass, when Solomon was old, that his wives turned away his heart after other gods: and his heart was not perfect with the Lord his God, as was the heart of David his father. For Solomon went after Ashtoreth the goddess of the Zidonians, and after Milcom the abomination of the Ammonites. And Solomon did evil in the sight of the Lord, and went not fully after the Lord, as did David his father. Then did Solomon build an high place for Chemosh, the abomination of Moab, in the hill that is before Jerusalem, and for Molech, the abomination of the children of Ammon. And likewise did he for all his strange wives, which burnt incense and sacrificed unto their gods. And the Lord was angry with Solomon, because his heart was turned from the Lord God of Israel, which had appeared unto him twice, And he commanded him concerning this thing, that he should not go after other gods: but he kept not that which the Lord commanded"* I Kings 11:4-10.

The word *angry* in verse nine is a word only used in the Hebrew of the Old Testament, signifying God's anger. It literally means *"to force one's self to be angry as with one loved"*. It occurs in this way only six times - Deuteronomy 1:37; 4:21; 9:8, 20; I Kings 11:9; II Kings 17:18.

What a tragedy! The wisest of kings the slave of pagan women and the builder of the Temple of the Lord an erecter of shrines of heathen idolatry.

Let us learn the lesson.

The sins of youth may have slain their thousands, but the sins of old age their tens of thousands. From such sins, good Lord, preserve us.

Then comes **Asa** the king of Judah.

He started well. The faithful Word puts on record *"And also Maachah his mother, even her he removed from being queen, because she had made an idol in a grove; and Asa destroyed her idol, and burnt it by the brook Kidron"* I Kings 15:10-13. Asa did right in the sight of the Lord therefore in the fulfilment of the promise his days were *"long in the land which the Lord God had given him"*.

He reigned 41 years, contemporary with seven kings of Israel.

Alas, however, in old age he turned from his God. The perils of growing old were too much for him. The record tells us *"And Asa in the thirty and ninth year of his reign was diseased in his feet, until his disease was exceeding great: yet in his disease he sought not to the Lord, but to the physicians"* II Chronicles 16:14.

God save us all from such an ending.

And what of his son **Jehoshaphat**.

It is recorded of Him *"And the Lord was with Jehoshaphat, because he walked in the first ways of his father David, and sought not unto Baalim; But sought to the Lord God of his father, and walked in his commandments, and not after the doings of Israel. Therefore the Lord stablished the kingdom in his hand; and all Judah brought to Jehoshaphat presents; and he had riches and honour in abundance. And his heart was lifted up in the ways of the Lord: moreover he took away the high places and groves out of Judah."* II Chronicles 17:3-6.

The exploits of Jehoshaphat and his deliverances were many for God was with him.

Alas, however, as he grew old he fell a prey to the perils of ageing. He had started his reign by strengthening himself against Israel (II Chronicle 17:1). Now he makes an affinity with the wicked Ahab and the still more wicked Jezebel by marrying off his son Jehoram to Athaliah their daughter. This was the road to ruin.

Jehoshaphat made three unequal yokes. 1, **Domestically**. The unequal yoke of marriage (II Chronicles 18:1 and I and II Chronicles 21:6); 2, **Militarily**, II Chronicles 18:2-34; 3, **Commercially**, II Chronicles 20:35-36

The consequences of these was that the land ran with blood. This was seen in our own history when James I married off his son Charles I to the Romanist Henrietta of France. England, Scotland and Ireland ran with blood, her husband Charles I lost his head and her son James II his throne.

No wonder the prophet of God Jehu came to Jehoshaphat with the awful indictment and judgment *"Shouldest thou help the ungodly and love them that hate the Lord? Therefore is wrath upon thee from before the Lord"* II Chronicles 19:3.

What an ending *"wrath upon thee from before the Lord."*

We need to flee from this wrath, the curse of falling to the perils of old age.

Further, **Joash** arrives on the scene.

He was just seven years old when he was enthroned to rule Judah after the wicked Athaliah, the daughter of Ahab and Jezebel, met her desserts through the skill of Jehoiada the High Priest.

Young King Joash started well his forty years reign. He repaired and re-opened the House of the Lord, the Temple of God. He was instrumental in a great revival of true religion.

When he grew older, however, he departed from His God. Listen to these sad words *"Now after the death of Jehoiada came the princes of Judah, and made obeisance to the king. Then the king hearkened unto them. And they left the House of the Lord God of their fathers, and served groves and idols: and wrath came upon Judah and Jerusalem for this their trespass"* II Chronicles 24:17-18.

Then he conspired in the killing of his gracious benefactor Jehoiaha's son Zechariah *"And the spirit of God came upon Zechariah the son of Jehoiada the priest, which stood above the people, and said unto them, Thus saith God, Why transgress ye the commandments of the Lord, that ye cannot prosper? because ye have forsaken the Lord, he hath also forsaken you. And they conspired against him, and stoned him with stones at the commandment of the king in the court of the house of the Lord. Thus Joash the king remembered not the kindness which Jehoiada his father had done to him, but slew his son. And when he died, he said, The Lord look upon it, and require it. And it came to pass at the end of the year, that the host of Syria came up against him: and they came to Judah and Jerusalem and destroyed all the princes of the people from among the people, and sent all the spoil of them unto the king of Damascus. For the army of the Syrians came with a small company of men and the Lord delivered a very great host into their hands, because they had forsaken the Lord God of their father. So they executed judgment against Joash. And when they were departed from him, (for they left him in great diseases,) his own servants conspired against him for the blood of the sons of Jehoiada the priest, and shew him on his bed, and he died; and they buried him in the city of David, but they buried him not in the sepulchres of the kings."* II Chronicles 24: 20-25

His bloody death was a tragic monument to the fact that he fell a prey to the perils of old age.

Let us all heed the trumpet blast of warning. Beware! Beware! Beware! of the perils of growing old.

The last person we want to look at is King **Uzziah** of Judah. How well he commenced! The record says *"And he did that which was right in the sight of the Lord, according to all that his father Amaziah did. And he sought God in the days of Zechariah, who had understanding in the visions of God: and as long as he sought the Lord, God made him to prosper. And he went forth and warred against the Philistines, and brake down the wall of Gath, and the wall of Jabneth, and the wall of Ashdod, and built cities about Ashdod, and among the Philistines. And God helped him against the Philistines, and against the Arabians that dwelt in Gur-baal, and he Mehunims. And the Ammonites gave gifts to Uzziah: and his name spread abroad even to the entering of Egypt; for he strengthened himself exceedingly"* II Chronicles 26:4-8

What a privilege he had to have the great prophet Zechariah for his royal chaplain!

But in growing old Uzziah grew rebelliouws. He fell by the perils of ageing. The sad chronicle reads *"But when he was strong, his heart was lifted up to his destruction: for he transgressed against the Lord his God, and went into the temple of the Lord to burn incense upon the altar of incense. And Azariah the priest went in after him, and with him fourscore priests of the Lord, that were valiant men: And they withstood Uzziah the king, and said unto him, It appertaineth not unto thee, Uzziah, to burn incense unto the Lord, but to the priests the sons of Aaron, that are concentrated to burn incense: go out of the sanctuary; for thou hast trespassed; neither shall it be for thine honour from the Lord God. Then Uzziah was wroth, and had a censer in his hand to burn incense; and while he was wroth with the priests, the leprosy even rose up in his forehead before the priests in the house of the Lord, from beside the incense altar. And Azariah the chief priest, and all the priests, looked upon him, and, behold, he was leprous in his forehead, and they thrust him out from thence; yea, himself hasted also to go out, because the Lord had smitten him. And Uzziah the king was a leper unto the day of his death, and dwelt in a several house, being a leper; for he was cut off from the house of the Lord: and Jotham his son was over the king's house, judging the people of the land."* II Chronicles 26:16-21.

Let us all behold the leper king and be warned that only by obedience to the Word of God, diligence at the Throne of God, and utter dependence on the Grace of God can we escape the perils of old age.

Remember: THE HOARY HEAD IS A CROWN OF GLORY, IF IT BE FOUND IN THE WAY OF RIGHTEOUSNESS (Proverbs 16:31)

A WORD OF HOPE AND ENCOURAGEMENT

> "Why those fears? Behold 'tis Jesus
> Holds the helm and guides the ship;
> Spread the sails and catch the breezes
> Sent to waft us through the deep,
> To the regions
> Where the mourners cease to weep.

> "Though the shore we hope to land on,
> Only by report is known,
> Yet we freely all abandon,
> Led by that report alone,
> And, with Jesus,
> Through the trackless deep move on.

> "Oh, what pleasures there await us;
> here the tempests cease to roar;
> There it is that they who hate us,
> Can molest our peace no more.
> Trouble ceases
> On that tranquil, happy shore."

5 The powerlessness of growing old

"As thy days so shall thy strength be" Deuteronomy 33:25

ALL OUR LIVES ARE LIMITED. Their boundaries are already set by the Sovereign God of heaven and earth, and beyond them we cannot pass.

There are none today like **Moses** who, at 120 years of age, could claim *his eye was not dim nor his natural force abated.*

There are none today like **Joshua** and **Caleb** who could declare at 85 years of age they were as strong then as when they were 40 years old.

Many of the great men of the Bible felt the weight of their years and growing old left them in a state of powerlessness.

What of **Isaac**? At 137 years he was *"old and his eyes were dim"* (Genesis 27:1). His half brother **Ishmael** died at that age. He himself thought he was going to die but he lived for another 43 years. (See Genesis 35:28). *"And the days of Isaac were a hundred and fourscore years."*

The powerlessness of growing old came to him early.

Jacob, his son, also grew old early. At one hundred and thirty years he felt the weight of his years and cried out pitifully to Pharaoh *"Few* *and evil have the days of the years of my life been."* (Genesis 47:9). Nevertheless, he had still seventeen years to live, for he died at 147 years of age.

So in reality he did not attain unto the age of his father Isaac.

Samuel knew the powerlessness of old age and confessed *"I am old and grey headed"* (I Samuel 12:2).

David's powerlessness in old age caught up with him, and in the day of battle with Goliath's son we read of him, *"David waxed faint"* (II Samuel 21:15).

Solomon's powerlessness in old age is tragically recorded. *"For it came to pass when Solomon was old that his wives turned away his heart after other gods and his heart was not perfect with the Lord his God"* (I Kings 11:4).

I wondered why some of God's saints master the powerlessness of old age while others are mastered by that powerlessness. Then I thought of the fact that we receive not because we ask not. Are we asking for power in our old age or are we merely prepared to submit to its paralysis?

Do we ask for healthy old age?

I remember receiving a promise from God years ago and I am revelling in its fulfilment today. *"He shall call upon me, and I will answer him: I will be with him in trouble; I will deliver him, and honour him. With long life will I satisfy him, and shew him my salvation."* Psalm 91:15-16

I. POWERLESSNESS TO REMEMBER

Memory is often wounded with the arrow of growing old. It no longer has its agility and invigoration. It falters and falls a prey to the aging process.

Failure to remember brings distress and frustration. It is strange, however, that in the failing of memory in the growing old process, the great spiritual experiences of life are fully and sweetly remembered with the greatest possible accuracy.

The day of confession and the sweet experience of our first meeting with the Saviour, His unfailing love and unfaltering care are never forgotten. They are so ingrained within our personality that they have become part of ourselves.

Yes, and when even in this spiritual sphere there is a faltering, how wonderful to know that if we lose the ability to remember God's great and exceeding precious promises, He never forgets them and will fulfil them in the same perfect way as if we still remembered them all.

Our God never fails nor is weary and He never slumbers nor sleeps.

Of our **past** God says, *"I took them by the hand to lead them out of the land of Egypt; because they continued not in my covenant, and I regarded them not, saith the Lord."* Hebrews 8:9.

Of our **present** God says, *"I ... will hold thine hand, and will keep thee, and give thee for a covenant of the people, for a light of the Gentiles."* Isaiah 42:6.

Of our **prospect** God says, *"I will never leave thee nor forsake thee (or never let go thine hand)"* Hebrews 13:5.

On 29th May, 1888, Dr Andrew Bonar wrote in his diary:

"My birthday. It came upon me with great awe, the thought that I have been now seventy-eight years in the world, and am now near the world to come. When I look round it is like a battlefield; many old friends gone; and then I see brethren like men wounded in the fight."

On the same day the year after, thinking specially of the time when he began to be assured that he had taken hold of Christ, he wrote: "

The Lord has enabled me to lean upon Christ day by day, for sixty years, or rather fifty-nine. He took hold of me that year (1830), and has never once left me in darkness as to my interest in Him all that time. I have been meditating upon His marvellous grace; and I see it in this light, viz: He promised that day I found Him that I would have rest in Himself always as I went along, and then nothing less than a whole eternity of blessedness. All this for accepting the Gift of Christ." These last eight words are a great sentence. You should learn them off by heart: *"All this for accepting the Gift of Christ."*

Is life worth living? **Yes if truth be true life is worth living, death worth dying too!**

II. POWERLESSNESS TO RETAIN

With the passing of the years we develop a powerlessness to retain our bodily strength.
The great Earl of Shaftesbury had this to say on his 83rd birthday.

"April 28th, 1884 - My birthday, and I have now struck the figure of *eighty-three*. It is wonderful, it is miraculous, with my infirmities, and even sufferings, of body, with sensible decline of mental application and vigour, I yet retain, by God's mercy, some power to think and to act. May He grant, for Christ's sake, that, to my last hour, I may be engaged in His service, and in the full knowledge of all that is around and before me! Cobden used to say of Disraeli - 'What a retrospect that man will have.' Retrospect must be terrible to every one who measures and estimates his hopes by the discharge of his duties here on earth ... But what are the prospects? They may be bright, joyous, certain, in the faith and fear of the Lord Jesus." - *The Earl of Shaftesbury's Diary.*

The year after, Lord Shaftesbury wrote:

"My birthday - this day I am eighty-four! God be merciful to me a sinner. A most terrible day to me for pain and irritation. But got, the Lord be praised, a birthday present. Some ladies, knowing how the Jewish Cyprus Colonisation Scheme pressed upon my mind, had collected £640 to clear the debt off, and presented it to me at Lady Eastlake's. The Lord be praised, and may His blessing descend on the contributors."

He died the following October. During his last illness he often asked his daughter to read the 23rd Psalm to him. His last words were "Thank you," addressed to a faithful man-servant.

III. POWERLESSNESS TO REMAIN

Here we have no continuing city but we seek one to come.

We are going down the valley, one by one,
With our faces towards the setting of the sun.
Down the valley where the mournful cypress grows,
Where the stream of death in silence onward flows.

We are going down the valley, one by one,
When the labours of life's weary day are done.
One by one, the toils of earth for ever past,
We shall stand upon death's river bank at last.

We are going down the valley, one by one,
Human comrade you and I will there have none,
May a tender hand thus hold us lest we fall
For only Christ can there be with us all.

Dr Joseph Hall, Bishop of Norwich, in a sermon preached in 1654, two years before he died, said:

"It hath pleased the providence of my God so to contrive it, that this very morning, fourscore years ago, I was born into this world. 'A great time since!' ye are ready to say; and so, indeed, it seems to you that look at it forward, but to me, that look at it past, it seems so short that it is gone like a tale that is told, or a dream by night, just like yesterday. It can be no offence for me to say that many of you who hear me this day are not like to see so many suns walk over your heads as I have done. Yea, what speak I of this? We are all tenants at will and for aught we know, may be turned out of these clay cottages at an hour's warning. Oh, then, what should we do, but, as wise farmers, who know the time of their lease is expiring and cannot be renewed, carefully and seasonably provide ourselves of a surer and more during tenure?"

Whatever happens to us, as powerlessness to remember, to retain, and to remain conquerors, let us not despair for the Will of God is always best.

Hark, my soul! It is the Lord;
'Tis thy Saviour, hear His word;
Jesus speaks, and speaks to thee:
'Say, poor sinner, lov'st thou Me?

'I delivered thee when bound,
And, when bleeding, healed thy wound;
Sought thee wandering, set thee right,
Turned thy darkness into light.

'Can a woman's tender care
Cease towards the child she bare?
Yes, she may forgetful be,
Yet will I remember thee.

'Mine is an unchanging love,
Higher than the heights above,
Deeper than the depths beneath,
Free and faithful, strong as death.

'Thou shalt see my glory soon,
When the work of grace is done;
Partner of My throne shall be:
Say, poor sinner, lov'st thou Me?'

Lord, it is my chief complaint
That my love is weak and faint;
Yet I love Thee, and adore;
O for grace to love Thee more!

- Bonar

"*Seeing then that we have a great high priest, that is passed into the heavens, Jesus the Son of God, let us hold fast our profession. For we have not an high priest which cannot be touched with the feeling of our infirmities; but was in all points tempted like as we are, yet without sin. Let us therefore come boldly unto the throne of grace, that we may obtain mercy, and find grace to help in time of need."* Hebrews 4:14-16

>Would we fall like the oak
>Decaying, to lie on the ground,
>The spirit alike with the body,
>Each sharing the one common mound?
>Or drop to the earth like the acorn
>And start a new life as before -
>To spring back again into childhood
>And renew our memories of yore?
>
>Would we take up the burden of trials,
>Contentedly carry them through,
>Rather than lie in inaction
>Forgetting the pleasures we knew?
>Yes, man, with no show of resistance
>Would travel the voyage once more,
>Were it not that we see in the distance
>A brighter life just on before.

6 The plague *of growing old*

"I, even I, only am left" I Kings 19:10

THE GREAT PLAGUE OF growing old is loneliness. How we wail with the ageing Elijah, "I, even I, only am left".

If we do not guard against this plague it will most certainly overcome us and make the evening shadows oh so hard with blackest night, instead of light tinged with the approaching dawn.

Loneliness is often self-inflicted. It was so with Elijah. Many of the seven thousand faithful worshippers of Jehovah who refused to kiss Baal's lips and bow to Baal's image would have been delighted to receive him into their homes. But Elijah, caught up with overwhelming loneliness, preferred to run alone into the arms of Jezebel the murderess. He should never have gone near Jezebel.

Then when Jezebel threatened him he fled with his servant to Judah, beyond Jezebel's reach into the southern kingdom. Not happy with his escape he forsook his servant, the one he needed most at this time of intense loneliness.

In him, he had one he could talk to, and how much he needed to talk and unburden his broken spirit, but instead he forsook his servant's company. Quickly he forgot how that same servant climbed Mount Carmel seven times at his command and brought him the good news of "the sound of abundance of rain".

Now he turned to the lonely road, to the forsaken, uninhabited wilderness, thus fuelling more fever to the anguish of his innermost soul.

There he found the juniper tree of despair and called on his God to kill him. He screamed out that he had had enough. (1 Kings 19:4).

As he lay and slept he had an angelic awakening. He was called upon to eat and drink. This he did and then went back to sleep again.

He was awakened the second time and summonsed to eat and drink again, because the journey of loneliness was too great for him.

Then, with fresh vigour, for forty days and nights he went on his way to Horeb, the mount of God.

But he was still not rid of his loneliness. The plague of old age was upon him. He wanted to die.

He tells God as he lies in the cave at Horeb that he only is left.

Commanded to stand on the mountain, he stood in the door of the cave and once again wailed, I, even I only am left. But God was not finished with Elijah. He had eleventh hour work to do. Notice that after God recommissioned him he gave the lie to Elijah's falsehood of loneliness. He said, *"Yet I have left me 7,000 in Israel all the knees which have not bowed unto Baal, and every mouth which hath not kissed him"* (I Kings 19:18).

A NAME IN THE SAND

> Alone I walked the ocean strand;
> A pearly shell was in my hand;
> I stooped and wrote upon the sand
> My name, the year, the day.
> As onward from the spot I passed,
> One lingering look behind I cast -
> A wave came rolling, high and fast,
> And washed my lines away.

And so, methought, 'twill shortly be
With every mark on earth from me;
A wave of dark oblivion's sea
Will sweep across the place
Where I have trod the sandy shore
Of time - and been, to be no more;
Of me, my name, the name I bore,
To leave no track nor trace.

And yet, with Him who counts the sands,
And holds the waters in His hands,
I know a lasting record stands
Inscribed against my name,
Of all this mortal part has wrought,
Of all this thinking soul has thought
And from these fleeting moments caught,
For glory or for shame
                    - HF Gould

The Lord Jesus came to destroy the plague of loneliness.

His Person and Purpose is Emmanuel - God with us. (Matthew 1:23).

O blessed Jesus help me to always know that Thou are ever with me and that Thou wilt never forsake me.

Someone has said that as we grow older three great enemies will beset us.

Enemy Number One - FEAR
But perfect love casts out all fear. Christ's passion is the answer to all fear.

Enemy Number Two - WORRY
But perfect peace casts out all worry. Christ's peace is the answer to all worry.

Enemy Number Three - LONELINESS
But the perfect presence casts out all loneliness. Christ Himself is the answer to loneliness. Emmanuel, God with us. If He is for us who, WHO, WHO can be against us?

Do not sob, my ageing friend, for the touch of the vanished hand and the sound of the voice that is still.

Christ's nail-pierced hand never vanishes nor is His voice ever still.

As the first New Testament book opens with Emmanuel - *God with us* so it closes with the same *"Lo I am with you alway"* (Matthew 28:20).

Alway - that means to the end of life and beyond death into the endlessness of His immediate personal presence in the Everlasting Ages.

This God, says the Psalmist, *is our God for ever and ever. He will be our guide even unto death* (Psalm 48:14).

The thrust of the verse is that God is his God for ever and ever, even unto death, over death and beyond death.

> About, above me evermore,
> Christ's gentle presence broods,
> He shares with me my silences,
> He fills my solitudes.
>
> His face, His form, I cannot see,
> No spoken word can hear,
> But with some finer sense of sound
> Do I perceive Him near.
>
> Oh how my heart within me burns!
> What ecstasy is mine,
> That He thus reaches unto me
> His comradeship divine.
>
> Are not these joys too sweet to last?
> May He not soon depart?
> "Lo I am with you all the days"
> He answereth my heart.

Alone

Alone, I stand beside Life's stream
And watch its surging splash and sheen,
And long for worlds unseen.

Alone, I note the ebb and flow-
The tides that come, the tides that go -
Of human weal and woe.

Alone, I pass on crowded street
By halls - whose throngs, with joy replete
Round friendship's altar meet.

Alone, I wander oft and muse
Along Thought's silent avenues,
As Duty's path I choose.

Alone, I sit at eventide
Midst Fancy's guests, who lurk and hide
In Memory's castle wide.

Alone, I count the sands of Time,
The shifting scenes of day's decline,
And turn to realms sublime.

Alone, I press Life's walks - alone!
As joys of other days have flown,
Yon heaven holds my own.

Alone, I tread upon the brink
Of Time's rough, rugged shores, and think
Beyond, "I'll pleasures drink".

Alone, ah yes, alone! I wait
A welcome through th' eternal gate
At close of earthly state.

Alone! yet not alone, I'll glide
Through angry waves which worlds divide,
With Jesus by my side.

Anna K. Thomas

The way to destroy the plague of loneliness is to recognise you are never alone.

The blessed Lord Jesus is ever near to bless and cheer in the darkest hour.

You will find Him in His Holy Word and at His Throne of Grace.

Cultivate the Company you have.

Be glad of all with whom you can talk and communicate. Be as pleasant as you can with them for pleasantness creates pleasantness.

Don't occupy them with your cares, occupy them with your comforts.

Make people want to come to you rather than you having to go to them.

Keep yourself occupied.

The tasks you need to do and the tasks that you like to do, engage in them both joyfully.

Give diligence to reading

Love the Bible. Take time to meditate. Learn to chew the cud.

Read again the books you enjoyed when you were young. A second read can be an absolute thrill.

Develop your prayer life.

Have frequent talks with the Master. I have never forgotten a hymn which I learned in childhood.

A little talk with Jesus
How it smooths the rugged road
How it seems to help me onward
When I faint beneath my load.
There's naught can yield the comfort
Like a little talk with Him.

Look forward to the Sabbath.

If at all possible be in your wonted place in the Lord's House. Speak to as many as you can. If you are shut in, get cassettes of the services and play them over at church times so that you can at long distance tune yourself into fellowship.

Get as many young people to visit you as you can.

Young people, yes even little children, admire the elderly and love to talk to them. Build bridges to them and by using those bridges they will bring blessings in their hand to you.

Above all, in everything give thanks.

Gratitude is the greatest sweetener. It is the honey of living.

Mr William Gosling, of Mansfield, Nottinghamshire, who had rung the bells in the belfry of the parish church for seventy-three years, celebrated his 86th birthday by joining with the other ringers in the Sabbath peals for the morning and evening services.

The late Captain Scott of Antarctic fame tells us in his book on the Voyage of the Discovery that when his men and he were pulling sledges they "learned to distinguish between the strong and the weak, and what was of more importance, between the willing and the lazy."

"The Bo'sun," he adds in another place, "has been pulling just behind me, and in some sympathy that comes through the traces I have got to know all about him. He has been suffering agonies in his back, yet he has never uttered a word of complaint, and when he knows my eye is on him he straightens up and pretends he is just as fit as ever." So on that 3rd August, 1913, I have no doubt a man with a critical ear might have been able to say he could tell that one of the players was a feeble old man with a slightly uncertain sense of time, but an Angel, accustomed to the music of the bells on the High Priest's robe, could have said, without looking at the players "There is some one pulling today whose heart is very full of love to God." For love is of God, and it cannot be hid, and a thrill would pass along the ropes that the very bell itself would feel and answer to.

To be a church bell-ringer is a high vocation. Every toll is a cry to people, "Behold, the Bridegroom." And the Spirit and the bride say, Come. And let him that heareth say, Come. And let him that is athirst come. And whosoever will, let him take the water of life freely.

Now, if ever there was a man whose name might seem to shut him out from having any lot or part in the concourse of sweet sounds, it was one with such a name as Gosling, for as gosling is a goose, and a goose's note is a cackle or a hiss. Yet, as it was the voices of the Geese in the temple of Juno that wakened Manlius and saved the capitol of Rome when the Gauls invaded Italy 2,300 years ago, so the sound of Mr Gosling's bell with its voice of thanksgiving and its call to prayer may touch an ear that the sermon of many a silver-tongued or golden-mouthed orator has missed.

God's Care

What am I that thou shouldst be
Mindful, O my God, of me,
Watching o'er me day by day,
Answering when I kneel to pray?

What am I that thou needst care
What I eat or drink or wear?
Matters it so much to thee
That I fed and clothed should be?

What am I that thou shouldst keep
Watch o'er me and never sleep,
Guiding, guarding, all my years,
Deepening joys and lessening fears?

What am I that thou must know
Every path where I may go;
That thy still, small voice should say,
"Walk ye in the narrow way"?

What am I that thou shouldst send
Thy Son to be my truest friend?
He who walked in Galilee
Has come to dwell and walk with me.

What am I that I should have
Endless life beyond the grave?
Why dost thou so much for me,
When I can do naught for thee?

Georgia C Elliott.

7 The potency
of growing old

ONE OF THE MIGHTIEST scriptural encouragements for more and greater spiritual success in the Lord's service for those growing old, is found in our Lord's parable of THE HIRING OF THE LABOURERS.

The famous Rev. Sylvester Horne, sometime member of Parliament and great London preacher at Whitefield's Tottenham Court Road Chapel (Grandfather of Rt. Hon. Wedgewood Benn MP) spoke to his friend about a sermon he had preached to old men and women and asked him to guess the text. His friend Kingscote Greenland said, 'Come unto me all ye that labour and are heavy laden.'

'No' replied the preacher.

'At eventide it shall be light?'

'No' responded Mr. Horne

'What was it?' asked Mr. Greenland

The preacher smiling replied, 'Matthew chapter twenty verse six, seven, eight and nine: *-And about the eleventh hour he went out, and found others standing idle, and saith unto them, Why stand ye here all the day idle?*

They said unto him, Because no man hath hired us. He saith unto them Go ye also into the vineyard; and whatsoever is right, that shall ye receive.

So, when even was come, the lord of the vineard saith unto his steward, Call the labourers, and give them their hire, beginning from the last unto the first.

And when they came that were hired about the eleventh hour, they received every man a penny.

Mark the eleventh hour!

The day was near its end but the power to gain in the last hours of that dying day the same reward as those who laboured the whole day is surely a spur to all those who are growing old. Here we have the potency of growing old.

Anyone who loses the motivation that the poet Browning wrote of:-

'Grow old along with me,
The best has yet to be
The last of life for which the first was made.
Our times are in God's hand,
Who saith, 'The whole I planned'
Youth shows but half; trust God; see all
Nor be afraid.'

will have a sad old age with all its real power lost - decapitated by a murdering non-expectancy.

It is absolutely true that

Our tasks may glow like jewels, or coruscate like gems,
But once their motive is withdrawn the deadly ebb begins;
We call it, 'hardened arteries,' 'pneumonia' and 'flu',
But men will die of heartbreak when they've nothing left to do.

Hunt the thought from your mind, heart and inward soul. Let it never be given house-room that your power to serve your God is over forever and all that is left for you is to throw a tantrum like Jonah under your gourd and cry out for the undertaker and grave-digger.

The other day in a second-hand bookstore I picked up a book called *THE QUEST OF THE SOUL,* by that old salvationist warrior Commissioner Brengle. He had just joined the 'over seventy club' and had this to say:-

"Seventy years are less than a pinpoint in the vastness of God's Eternity, but they are a long, long time in the life of a man. When I was a child a man of seventy seemed to me to be as old as the hills. I stood in awe of him. No words could express how venerable he was. When I looked up to him it was like looking up to the snowy, sun-crowned, storm-swept heights of great mountains.

And now, having lived threescore years and ten, I feel as one who has scaled a mighty mountain, done an exploit, or won a war. What toil it has involved! What dangers have been met and overcome! What dull routine; what thrilling adventure! What love, what joy and sorrow, what defeats and victories, what hopes and fears; what visions and dreams yet to be fulfilled! And the River not far away, yet to be crossed. "My soul, be on thy guard!" I remember and marvel."

• • •

"And yet I feel I am but a child. At times I feel as frisky as a boy and have stoutly to repress myself to keep from behaving frivolously as a boy, and I hear my friend and brother, mentor and companion of half a century, Paul, saying: 'Aged men be sober, grave, temperate' (Titus 2:2)

Then again I feel as old as I am. The leaden weight of seventy years presses heavily upon me.

I look back and it seems like centuries since I was a carefree little lad; then some vivid memory will leap up within me, and the seventy years seem like a tale of yesterday and I am again a "wee little boy with the tousled head," playing around the flower-embowered cottage in the tiny village by the Blue River where I was born.

The average age of man is much less than seventy years, so I am a leftover from a departed generation. But while the snows of seventy winters are on my head, the sunshine of seventy summers is in my heart.

The fading, falling leaves of seventy autumns solemnise my soul, but the resurrection life upspringing in flower and tree, the returning song birds, the laughing, leaping brooks and swelling rivers, and the sweet, soft winds of seventy springtimes gladden me."

•••

"When I consider the vanishing darkness, the toppling thrones, the crumbling empires, the fallen crowns, the outlawed tyrannies, the mastery of nature's secrets, the harnessing of her exhaustless energies, the penetration of all lands with the story and light of the Gospel, which I have witnessed in my day, I can but feel that I was born at the beginning of the end of the Dark Ages.

But, while the light increases and widens, the darkness still comprehends it not. And while God's 'truth is marching on', evil men and seducers wax worse, become more self-conscious and class-conscious and organise and mass themselves to fight against God and His Christ and His saints and soldiers more subtly and determinedly than at any time since the days of the Roman persecutions and the Spanish Inquisition."

•••

"I do not expect the love of the Father, the eternal intercession of the risen and enthroned Son, the wise and loving ceaseless ministry of conviction, conversion, regeneration and sanctification of the Holy Ghost, the prayers, and preachings and sacrifice and holy living of the soldiers of Jesus and saints of God, to fail. Jesus is even now leading on His hosts to victory, Hallelujah!

I cannot always, if ever, comprehend His great strategy. My small sector of the vast battlefield may be covered with smoke and thick darkness. The mocking foe may be pressing hard, and comrades may fear and falter and flee, and the enemy may apparently triumph as he did when Jesus died, and when the martyrs perished in sheets of flame, by the sword and headman's axe, mauled by the lion's paw, crunched by the tiger's tooth and slain by the serpent's fang. But the enemy's triumph ever has been and ever will be short, for Jesus is leading on and up, ever on, ever up, never backward, never downward, always forward, ever toward the rising sun. Revivals, resurrection life and power, are resident in our religion. A dead church, a dead Salvation Army corps, may, when we least expect, flame with revival fire, for Jesus, though unseen, is on the battlefield, and He is leading on. 'Lo, I am with you alway, even unto the end of the world' (Matt. 27:20)

In the lonely and still night, while others sleep, He stirs some longing soul to sighs and tears and strong cryings and wrestling prayer. He kindles utter, deathless devotion in that soul, a consuming jealously for God's glory, for the salvation of men, for the coming of the Kingdom of God; and in that lonely and still night out of that travail, the agony of spirit, mingled with solemn joy, a revival is born. Behold, 'the kingdom of God cometh not with observation' (Luke 17:20). There may be no blast of trumpets, no thunder of drums, no flaunting of flags. The revival is born in the heart of some lonely, longing, wrestling, believing, importunate man or woman who will give God no rest, who will not let Him go without His blessing. Brighteyed, golden-haired, rosy-cheeked dolls can be made by machinery and turned out to order, but living babies are born of sore travail and death agony. So revivals may be simulated, trumped up, made to order but not so do revivals begotten by the Holy Ghost come."

• • •

"Though retired I must still 'watch ... in all things, endure afflictions, do the work of an evangelist, and make full proof of [my] ministry' (2 Tim. 4:5). For the solemn day of accounting is yet to come - coming surely, swiftly - when I must render an account of my stewardship; when the final commendations or condemnations shall be spoken; when the great prizes and rewards will be given, and the awful deprivations and dooms will be announced.

Apostles though they were, Peter and Paul never lost their awe of that day; nor must I, for Jesus said: 'Many will say to Me in that day, Lord,

Lord, have we not prophesied in Thy name? and in Thy name have cast out devils? and in Thy name have done many wonderful works? And then will I profess unto them, I never knew you: depart from me' (Matthew 7: 22,23)

Remembering these words I gird my armour closer, grip my sword, and watching, praying, marching breast forward, I sing,

> My soul, be on thy guard!
> Ten thousand foes arise;
> The hosts of Hell are pressing hard
> To draw thee from the skies.
>
> Ne'er think the battle won,
> Nor lay your armour down:
> The fight of faith will not be done
> Till thou obtain the crown!

It is a fight of faith, and faith is nourished by the word of the Lord, to which I return daily for my portion and am not denied. Hallelujah!"

• • •

"My father-in-law lived to be nearly ninety, and he said, 'As men grow old they become either sweet or sour.' He ripened sweetly and became more and more gracious in his old age. I want to be like that.

> Let me grow lovely, growing old,
> So many fine things do;
> Laces, and ivory, and gold
> And silks need not be new;
>
> And there is healing in old trees;
> Old streets a glamour hold;
> Why may not I, as well as these,
> Grow lovely, growing old?

- From Brengle's Quest of the Soul

Remember this life is but the cradle of the other. Of what importance then are illness and age, time and death?

They can be either stages, in the eternal transformations or eternal disfigurations, which have their commencements here on earth.

The evening of life bears in its hand either the darkest of lanterns or the brightest lights.

The phrase "good old age" is most interesting as it occurs in the Holy Scriptures.

Abram was given this promise in Genesis 16:15 *"And thou shalt go to thy fathers in peace: thou shalt be buried in a **good old age**."* What a promise this was for Abram. He had already refused the riches of the King of Sodom and had received God Almighty as his exceeding great reward. Then he offered the sacrifice of God's direction and, like Adam, a deep sleep came upon him. When Adam arose out of his sleep he had a bride, when Abram arose out of his sleep he had a more sure word of prophecy of the seed already promised in its history and destiny.

The expression occurs the second time in Genesis 25:8 when the promise of its first mention is fulfilled *"Then Abraham gave up the ghost and died in **good old age**, an old man full of years; and was gathered to his people."*

The same expression is used of the Judge Gideon. Judges 8:32 *"And Gideon, the son of Joash, died in **good old age** and was buried in the sepulchre of Joash his father in Ophrah of the Abiezrites."*

The expression occurs in the life of David the king. I Chronicles 29:28 *"And he died in **good old age** full of days, riches and honour, and Solomon his son reigned in his stead."*

So the Father of the nation, the Judge of the nation and the King of the nation had potency in their old age, it being described as *good old age*.

These are the only three in Scripture whose old age is described by this expression.

Good old age indeed!

There are others mentioned who were notably blessed in their old age.

Jacob begat Joseph, described in Genesis 37:3 as *"the son of his **old age**"* and Joseph's younger brother, Benjamin, is also described as *"the child of his **old age**"* (Genesis 44:20).

Sarah's son, Isaac, the promised seed of Abraham was also *"a son of old age"* (Genesis 21:2).

Ruth's husband, Boaz, was to Naomi, Ruth's mother in law, *"a nourisher of her **old age**"* (Ruth 4:15). Elizabeth bore John the Baptist in *"her **old age**"* (Luke 1:36).

There is certainly a power in old age which makes it **good** old age and **fruitful** old age. The Psalm 92:13 states *"THEY SHALL STILL BRING FORTH FRUIT IN OLD AGE."*

God is the God of the old aged. Does He not say, *"Hearken unto me, O house of Jacob, and all the remnant of the house of Israel, which are borne by me from the belly, which are carried from the womb: And even to your **old age** I am he; and even to hoar hairs will I carry you: I have made and I will bear; even I will carry, and will deliver you."* (Isaiah 46:3-4).

If ever a man gave a remarkable demonstration of power in old age it was the great and wonderfully unique man of God, George Müller.

The followings eloquent testimonies to the potency of old age are from *The Morning Watch* 1914, a half-penny paper edited by a famous genius, the Reformed Presbyterian Minister of Greenock *Rev J P Struthers*.

On his 90th birthday, 27th September, 1895, George Müller, the founder of the Orphan Homes at Bristol, told the friends who came to see him with their good wishes, that he attributed the very great happiness he had had for 69 years and ten months to two things: first, he had striven by God's grace to have a good conscience, not wilfully going on in any cause he knew to be contrary to the mind of God; and, secondly, he had been a lover of the Holy Scriptures. For a long time he had read the whole Bible right through, four times every year, striving to apply it to his own heart by meditation and prayer.

In these days when we are all saying as much ill of Prussia as we can, it is good for us to be told that it was in that country this wonderful man was born. When he was a young lad he seems to have been about as bad as he could be. He stole money, for instance, more than once. When he was sixteen he was sent to jail for four weeks for defrauding the keeper of the hotel in which he had taken lodgings. But when he was twenty a fellow student took him one day to a prayer meeting that was held in the house of a Christian tradesman named Wagner. "Come as often as you like," said his kindly host, "house and heart are open to you." That was the first thing that impressed him, and the next was the kneeling down to pray of one of the company named Keyser, a man who was afterwards a Missionary of the London Bible Society in Africa. "This kneeling down," said Müller afterwards, "made a deep impression on me, for I had never before seen any one on his knees, nor had I ever myself prayed on my knees."

He died in 1898, having built in the course of his life five enormous houses for orphans which cost £115,000, all of which, as well as the £26,000 (that is £500 a week) needed annually, he got by voluntary contributions in answer to prayer. In all, he received during the seventy years of his active life £1,5000,000 of which £250,000 went to missions and the circulation of the scriptures, the rest going to the feeding and training of 123,000 orphans whom he sent out into the world. When he died he left property valued at £160 9s 4d, of which £60 3s 4d was in money.

The two things that chiefly led him into the great work of his life were, first, the example of August Hermann Francke - a German - 1663-1727, the man who, finding one day that he had the enormous sum of about £2 at his disposal, felt he was bound to do something good with it, and forthwith started a school for poor children; and the second thing was that text in Psalm 68: 5-6, *"A father of the fatherless, and a judge of the widows, is God in his holy habitation. God setteth the solitary in families: he bringeth out those which are bound with chains: but the rebellious dwell in a dry land."*

Between his 70th and 87th year Mr Müller travelled over 200,000 miles, in 42 different countries, preaching the Gospel, and saw hundreds upon hundreds of souls converted to God.

It was a word of Mr Müller's that led Mr Hudson Taylor to found the China Inland Mission.

Our venerable brother, whose very presence is a testimony for God, has preserved, in his old age, in travelling throughout all lands, bearing witness to the faithfulness of the Lord God, in whom he had trusted so long, and so fully. Seeing he must be in his eighty-fourth year, we can hardly expect that he should do much more; but it is delightful to observe how strength has been given him unto this present. His esteemed wife, by answering his letters, and other helpful service, makes his work more easy, and thus keeps his mind more free for labour. He has thus time for prayer and preaching, and bearing witness to the many who gather about him. It was a great means of grace to hear and see our friend, some ten years ago, at Mentone. It was not only his word, but the man himself that spake to our heart; for he has tried and proved the promises of God.

This was good old age alright.

Let us listen to another witness, the Earl of Cranborn:

"October 1, 1902. It seems a great age that I have attained to, 88, and yet at times I feel a buoyancy which seems almost youthful. Age, however, imposes its needful restrictions, and I strive to keep within them, and thank God for health and strength such as are vouchsafed - intelligence - the senses preserved - a real home of affection - Laus Deo!" (Praise be to God). - Earl of Cranborn's Diary. He kept his diary till January, 1906, and died one month after closing his 92nd year.

"I entered into the 90th year of my age," wrote John Mill of Shetland in his Diary, Feb. 23rd, 1801, "and may say with the good Patriarch Isaac, I know not the day of my death, yet desire, with good Job, to wait patiently God's best time, etc."

What infinitude there is in that "etc."! Might one not say with all reverence that if all the things that are involved in it should be written every one, even the world itself could not contain the books that should be written?

A few months before, he writes: "Our trade at present employs 10,000 vessels and 120,000 seamen. Exports valued at 27 millions sterling. Imports at 21 million sterling. Yet the kingdom is burdened with taxes, whereof great sums are given to powers on the Continent for carrying on war against the French; nay, so infatuated are our statesmen as to send armies to attack them there after several fruitless attempts lately at Holland and Ostend, to the great expense of our nation in blood and treasure, which we had no concern with while masters of the sea ... Imperial Parliament begins January 22, 1801. Malta is taken from the French, and General Abercromby goes there with an army, to fall on the French left in Egypt. The yellow fever rages at Cadiz in Spain, and, as a plague, sweeps off multitudes."

And then follows a passage that might have been written by an old Cameronian Minister: "Tis said that the present King George, tho' one of the best Kings that ever were in Great Britain, is now to assume the title of King of the United Kingdom of Great Britain and Ireland, Defender of the Faith, and of the United Church of England and Ireland. On earth the title of Supreme Head, sacred Majesty, belong only to the Lord Jesus Christ, to whom all power in heaven and earth is given"

On December 29, 1896, Mr Gladstone wrote: "My long and tangled life this day concludes its 87th year. My father died four days short of that term. I know of no other life so long in the Gladstone family, and my profession has been that of politician, or, more strictly, minister of State, an extremely short-lived race when their scene of action has been in the House of Commons, Lord Palmerston being the only complete exception. In the last twelve months my eyes and ears may have declined, but not materially. The occasional contraction of the chest is the only inconvenience that can be called new …

"The blessings of family life continue to be poured in the largest measure upon my unworthy head. Even my temporal affairs have thriven. Still old age is appointed for the gradual loosening and succeeding snapping of the threads."

Evening Time Best

There are who say that evening time is best,
When everything in nature sinks to rest;
Although the morning hour is passing fair,
With warmth and beauty springing everywhere,
And hope abrooding in the balmy air,
And drowning with glad music anxious care,
Still many hold that evening is best.

Full well I know that evening time is best
To one aweary and in need of rest;
But surely morning, with its rosy light

Asweeping back the curtains of the night,
Until the earth, all beautiful and bright,
Bursts forth in one grand anthem of delight,
To youth and joyous childhood is the best.

But oh, to me the evening time is best!
For I am tired, and I sigh for home;
I long beneath my Father's roof to rest,
To lean my head upon my Brother's breast;
I watch the sun declining to the west,
Rejoicing that the evening time is come!

— Mrs Lou S. Bedford.

The Christian's Prayer

While closing day leaves something still to do,
Some deeper truth to learn, some gift to gain,
Let me with cheerful mind my task pursue,
And, thankful, glean the fragments that remain.

From distant years if tearful memories rise,
Dear scenes and faces known on earth no more,
Unchanging Friend, to Thee I turn mine eyes,
And all my sadness in Thy bosom pour.

Draw nearer to me: let these days be blessed
By thoughts familiar with the things to be;
And varying feelings find their perfect rest
In one sweet Hope - to be at Home with Thee.

— Canon Bergard

8 The prospects *of growing old*

OLD AGE, OF NECESSITY, because of the guilt of man, has its weaknesses, its limitations, its perils and its regrets.

Old age, of necessity, because of the grace of God, has its strengths, its openness, its hopes and its prospects.

Scripture excites in us longing for heaven by giving us a prospective view of *"what must it be to be there"*.

Heaven's creations are so dazzling - *eye hath not seen;*

Heaven's communications are so delightful - *ear hath not heard;*

Heaven's coronations are so divine - *neither hath it entered into the heart of man;*

that all we can say God has, is prepared them for those who love Him.

Heaven is the bottom of the Divine Love.

Heaven is the surface of the Divine Love.

Heaven is the boundary of the Divine Love - of the love of Father, Son and Holy Ghost - the Eternal Three in One and the Eternal One in Three.

No wonder Paul, having been caught up into the third heaven, (the first heaven is the heaven of the birds, the second heaven is of the stars and the third is the heaven of God Himself) had an overwhelming desire to depart and be with Christ, for where Jesus is 'tis heaven there.

There are two ways of getting to that Heaven of heavens. Both have examples recorded in the Scriptures, one by death, as the first man, Adam, and two, by being caught up as Enoch, the seventh from Adam.

The New Testament never tells us to wait for death, but it does tell us to wait for the second coming of the Lord.

No saint is ever afraid of falling asleep in Christ or being caught up to meet Christ, for why should they? Both will be immediate glory! *"But I would not have you to be ignorant, brethren, concerning them which are asleep, that ye sorrow not, even as others which have no hope. For if we believe that Jesus died and rose again, even so them also which sleep in Jesus will God bring with him. For this we say unto you by the word of the Lord, that we which are alive and remain unto the coming of the Lord shall not prevent them which are asleep. For the Lord himself shall descend from heaven with a shout, with the voice of the archangel, and with the trumph of God: and the dead in Christ shall rise first: Then we which are alive and remain shall be caught up together with them in the clouds, to meet the Lord in the air: and so shall we ever be with the Lord. Wherefore comfort one another with these words."* I Thessalonians 4:13-18.

Meeting the Lord in the air is an absolute certainty for every believing soul but death is only a possibility. Even those who are old may not see death but be caught up alive. *Even so come Lord Jesus.*

The following story is told by Henry Durbanville in his great little book *"The best is yet to be"*;

'A very sick man asked his physician one day if he was likely to recover, and the doctor answered that, while it was quite possible, a second or a third attack, such as he had had, usually proved fatal. 'Doctor,' said the patient very earnestly, 'I am afraid to die. Tell me what lies on the other side.' 'I do not know,' replied the medical man. 'What,' said the other, 'you, a Christian man, and yet you do not know what is on the other side!'

'The doctor at this point was holding the handle of the door, from the other side of which came sounds of scratching and whining. Opening the door, his big, lovely dog immediately bounded into the room, showing great delight at being once again in the presence of his master for whom he had been waiting outside. Turning to the patient, the doctor said: 'Do you see this dog? He has never been in this room before; he didn't know what it was like inside. But he knew his master was here; and when the door was opened he sprang in without fear.' The speaker continued: 'I know little of what lies on the other side of death; but I do know that my Master is there; and when He opens the door I shall pass in not only fearlessly but gladly.'

Listen to this:

"I love to think of heaven; its cloudless light,
Its tearless joys, its recognitions and its fellowships
Of love and joy unending. But when my soul anticipates
The sight of God Incarnate, wearing on His hands,
And feet, and side, the marks of the wounds
Which He for us on Calvary endured,
All heaven beside is swallowed up in this -
And He, Who was my hope of Heaven below,
Becomes the glory of my Heaven above."

Coming to the end of reading my Bible through for 1997. I was struck once more with Zechariah 14:7 *"It shall come to pass that at eventide it shall be light."*

What a glorious surprise, when the flowers have closed their eyes because of the darkness of eventide, when foxes have slunk into their holes because of sunset, when the birds of the air have returned to their nests because the night has come, suddenly, gloriously, mysteriously, supernaturally, it is noontide and a glorious dawning. Such is the dawning of heaven.

When I was a child I fought off going to sleep. My mother would pick me up, cuddle me in her arms and sing me over to sleep and carry me upstairs. I knew nothing about it until I awoke upstairs in the morning. For me eventide had become light! What a glorious prospect old age can have of heaven!

The other day I happened to lift a copy from my library shelves of *The Christian World Pulpit* for the year 1902.

In it I came across a most interesting and illuminating sermon by *Theodore L Cuyler DD* a very prominent American Presbyterian minister who was a warm personal friend of the Prince of English preachers, the great CH Spurgeon. The Schaff-Herzog Encyclopedia gives this note about Dr Cuyler.

'**Cuyler, Theodore Ledyard, DD** (Princeton, 1866), Presbyterian; b. at Aurora, Cayuga County, NY, Jan. 10, 1822; graduated at the College of New Jersey, 1841, and at Princeton Theological Seminary, 1846; became stated supply at Burlington, NJ, 1846; pastor of the Third Presbyterian Church, Trenton, 1849; of the Marketstreet Reformed Church, New York City, 1853; and of the Lafayette-avenue Presbyterian Church, Brooklyn, NY, 1860. His church reported in 1885 a membership of 2,012. He has contributed 2,700 articles to leading religious papers of America and Europe, and been active in temperance work. He is the author of *Stray Arrows*, New York, 1852, new ed. 1880; *The Cedar Christian*, 1858, new ed. 1881; *The Empty Crib: A Memorial*, 1868; *Heart Life*, 1871; *Thought Hives*, 1872; *Pointed Papers for the Christian Life*, 1879; *From the Nile to Norway*, 1881; *God's Light on Dark Clouds*, 1882; *Wayside Springs from the Fountain of Life*, 1883; *Right to the Point*, 1884; *Lafayette-avenue Church*, 1885 (exercises connected with the celebration of the 25th anniversary of his pastorate, April 5 and 6, 1885).

Dr Cuyler's sermon is upon the text I have just quoted, that at eventide it shall be light.

The uniqueness of the sermon is that it was preached by Dr Cuyler in Lafayette Avenue Presbyterian Church on Sunday, January 12th on his celebration of his eightieth birthday. The sermon illustrates the prospects of growing old in a most unusual and interesting way.

Here are some extracts:

"Praise God from whom all blessings flow" is the song of my old heart in singing this happy morning which shines with seven-fold the brightness of yonder sun. This is a great Sabbath to me, I can assure you. My cup runneth over: and taking that full cup with thanksgiving I have come once more to this beloved church, to face this beloved flock to bring to you such a message as I trust the Living God will permit me now to offer. I shall not inflict any historical discourse on you, nor indulge to any great degree in personal reminiscence. I would rather come to you as I have always come, that is, to bring a simple Gospel message to you all. The text I have chosen I think may not be inappropriate to a message at fourscore.

"The text, which I now invite you to consider, you will find in Zechariah xiv. 7: "At evening time it shall be light." Despair is demoralising; fear is deadening; doubt is debilitating; hope, after all, comes to sit down with us when we are tempted and troubled, and when no relief would otherwise break upon our dreary path, and sheds a light like the stars in the sky, and we can push gratefully and cheerfully forward. God's word is a wonderful book in many respects; and one is that it addresses itself, not to our fears, but continually to our hopes. It never appeals to despair, but always to the possibility and expectation of better, better things to come. Scores of promises have floated out from this pulpit to you, like life-boats to those who have felt as if they were sinking beneath the waves. Many, many a time I have been permitted to hoist lantern texts to those passing through dark waters and the shadow of death. Now this morning I bring such a one from that cheerful old prophet who describes the day when Jerusalem, after passing through a time of persecution and wrong, should once more come to be a happy capital, her "children playing in the streets."

A COMFORTING WORD

"I am well aware that this text is regarded by my friend Meyer, and probably by the preacher who will occupy this pulpit tonight, as it was also by Moody, as prophetic of the Millennium. They regard it as a foretokening of the day when Christ shall stand again on the Mount of Olives, and God's peculiar people shall be gathered, and Jerusalem shall have a fresh outburst of glory. I shall not enter into that discussion. It would be utterly inappropriate. Of that day and hour no man knoweth but the Father. It is known to Jehovah, and that is enough. Whether you and I can tell the time and place of triumph of our blessed Lord, matters little, so that we consecrate ourselves to the great and joyful work of helping forward the coming of the kingdom. This text is a perfect gem. Like a diamond, it has many sides which will bear turning. Is it not the province of a diamond to shine in a dark room? So this text throws out brightness and joy to many an eye that is full of weeping and sorrow because of bereavement. Now the very essence of hope lies in this, that it is an expectation of better things, and kindles our hearts and minds to an expectation of blessing for this life and for the life to come. Sometimes the word hope in the Bible signifies a trust - as when we are told that hope in Christ is "as an anchor sure and steadfast, entering within the veil."

"Some persons may have come up here this morning who have brought trouble and disquiet of heart, or some loss, it may be, that has caused you sorrow and anxiety. There never can be an assemblage such as this without some hearts in it needing an uplift right from the throne of God. I come, therefore, this morning to bring you these words of cheer, because it may be a needful message to many a one in this congregation. Perhaps your pathway in the days gone by has been dark and dreary, like "Christian" at the Hill Difficulty in Bunyan's "Pilgrim's Progress," and you have gone from running to walking, from walking to climbing on your hands and knees.

"Have not some of us had experiences in the glorious Alps, when, on nearly reaching the top, we have been surrounded by clouds, mist filled the air, the tempest hurtled around us, and we sat down utterly disappointed in our hope of a glorious view and ready to wail with despair at a lost day, a lost prospect, a lost joy. But by-and-by a strong wind swept the heavens and revealed the beauty of the skies! There stood the white throne of the Monte Rosa, and yonder the magnificent Matterhorn, and as the evening sun bathed it in rosy glory we have stood lost in admiration. "At evening time it was light." Have not you and I had experiences in the past like that? Ah! we have, and realised the blessed hope. We cannot give up in despair, even in times of trial. Many are the experiences of this kind, I say, in the history of God's people.

"Look at poor old Jacob, bewailing the fate of his dead: "All these things are against me; I will go down into the grave unto my son mourning." Wait a minute! The caravan is coming! Glorious news! His sons returning, bring full sacks of corn to Jacob and his family. At evening time to the old man it is light- it is light! If you and I have no stormy days we never can enjoy the bright ones. If we never have any dark mists, we never can enjoy the outburst of the sunshine from behind the clouds. In the darkest moment Faith strikes a light and cheers the faint.

"Fear not, fear not, at evening time it shall be light. Think it not strange concerning the fiery trial that has tried you, as though some strange thing happened unto you; only keep pushing on, higher, higher, higher every hour, assured that you will get above the lower cloud and be bathed with the effulgence directly from the skies. After all, the Christian life is a walk of faith from beginning to end. God never deceives His children. There is never a broken promise in all the history of God's Church, not one. All things work together for good to them that love Him. He says, "I will make the darkness to be light before you, the crooked things straight. These things will I do for you." Very often our poor hearts feel

> The way is dark, my Father,
> Cloud on cloud is gathering thick before me,
> And loud the thunders roar above me. See, I stand
> Like one bewildered. Father, take my hand,
> And through the gloom lead safely home Thy child.
> Listen! Back comes the answer:
> The day comes fast, My child. And it shall be
> Not one step longer than is best for thee.
> Cling close to Me, and ev'ry spectral cloud
> Of fear shall vanish. I will take thy hand,
> And then at evening time it shall be light,
> My child."

In the previous chapter we listened to Dr. Cuyler as he celebrated his eightieth birthday by preaching to his congregation.

The aged preacher finished his great sermon thus:-

"I ask you to listen to these words, written by perhaps the grandest philanthropist of the nineteenth century, William Wilberforce, the champion of the Bible and of foreign missions, who at last went up to heaven carrying millions of broken fetters to lay them before God. Listen to Wilberforce. He says:-

'I sometimes understand why my life has been spared so long. It is to prove that I can be just as happy since I lost my worldly fortune as when I possessed it.' (Wilberforce suffered great pecuniary losses). Sailors, it is said, on a voyage at sea drink to the friends astern till they get half over, then to the friends ahead for the rest of the voyage. We may discern friends ahead for many a year. He was getting nearer home and at evening it was light.

"And I might add just here, coming back to this dear spot, that I miss from these pews some of the most loved faces I ever knew, and I think of where they are this morning. I stand and say, 'Friends ahead! Friends ahead! Ere long perhaps your old pastor will join you in the song before the throne!'

"Is the end of every life bright? No, no, no! Friend, it will not be light with you if you attempt the terrible experiment of spending it without Jesus Christ. A Christless life, I repeat it, a Christless life brings at last a hopeless soul, a homeless soul, and a heavenless soul! When you meet Him He will say, 'I called you and ye refused: I stretched out My pierced hands and ye would not regard it; henceforth depart from me, for ye would not have eternal life.' Oh, if there be in this assembly this morning one solitary man, woman or child, that has lived up to this day of January, 1902 without Christ, I beg you, and God speaking through me, I entreat you today to accept this great salvation.

A HAPPY ENDING

"And now my last thought. To those without Christ life ends oft in darkness and perhaps in despair. Yet for Christ's own people the close of life may be among its most precious, its most joyous, its most delightful of all experiences throughout life's long journey. I love to recall as there comes before me the thousands of God's people that I have known, how beautifully God has fulfilled the promise of my text, 'At evening time there shall be light.' I recall this morning an experience I once had in a house not far from this sanctuary. Pastors may gather more from their people than they give to them. Some of the best teaching I have ever had has come from the lips of my own flock who were verifying and substantiating the power of an indwelling Christ. I recall an hour spent some years ago in a room where one of God's faithful handmaidens was closing life with a most excruciating malady. The end was coming near, I stood to hear a far off token word from the eternities and catch a foregleam of the throne. I shall never forget the pathos of her utterance when she repeated,

> Abide with me, fast falls the eventide.
> Hold Thou Thy cross before my closing eyes;
> Shine through the gloom, and point me to the skies
> Heaven's morning breaks, and earth's vain shadows flee:
> *In life, in death, O Lord, abide with me.*

"You know that toward evening often the sun shines with a peculiar sweetness and radiance. Late in the afternoon the atmosphere seems to have lost its impurity and is strangely clear, and in that evening light we gaze as it were into the heavens. So it is with the departing Christian - every hour gaining new discoveries, every hour enlarging knowledge. Scientific discovery is a continual movement out of the unknown into the known. During my fourscore years I have seen the evidence, the splendid triumph of the principle of the continual invasion of the region of the unknown by the lamp of scientific discovery. Precisely so in religion. We are passing all the time out of the unknown into the known. Here we see though a glass dimly, then face to face. O what mysteries will be cleared up then. What problems will be solved! What puzzles will be explained! What apparently strange acts and orderings of Providence will become just as clear as the noon day. And then, O heavenly, everlasting discovery! We shall need no Bible then. It is here we need the guidebook. We shall not need to read God's Word. We had God's Word, and God's mercies, and prayer, outside the gate; we have no need for them any longer. God gave them here for the journey. When we get there we experience an eternal flooding of light and glory. Now we look at God's Providences, and it is like looking on the rude, rough side of a tapestry, rugged, ragged, unexplained, sometimes revolting. We need to turn it to God's side. In eternity we come upon God's side of the tapestry. There are the magnificent marchings of Providence. Heaven grant that you and I may study God's Providence, redemption, and Christ, where at evening time the light of earth shall give place to the morning of glory. There shall be no night there, no funeral processions, no broken hearts, no distress, disappointments, despair, or death. All these will be dropped when we pass through the gates into the City.

"Friends, are you ready? Am I ready? Are you ready to live? that is best of all; then you will be ready to depart when the hour shall come. Oh, to be ready when the time shall come! Oh, to be ready, ready to tread the last road to where the glorious crown awaits!"

> No chains to sever
> That earth has twined,
> No spell to loosen
> That sin would bind,
> No fitting shadows
> To dim the light,
> When heavenward pinions
> Are winged for flight
> But sweetly, gently
> To pass away,
> Out of the twilight
> Into the day -
> The glorious day!
> The endless, endless Day!
> What an ending which never ends!

Oh! What shall I write of Emmanuel's Land and City. Peter speaks of it as *'an inheritance, incorruptible, that fadeth not away, reserved in heaven, for you.'*

Note carefully its five characteristics:-

I. ITS IMMENSITY - 'AN INHERITANCE'

The inheritance of all the saints of all the ages - there never was an inheritance so immense before. There can never be an inheritance to compare with its immensity in the future. Oh the length of it! Oh the breadth of it! Oh the height of it!

Man's measuring instruments faint at the very shadow of it. They are stricken with the paralysis of their own impotency.

II. ITS INCORRUPTIBILITY - 'INCORRUPTIBLE'

Corruption is the brandmark of sin and the sure fruit of iniquity.

Where there is no sin there can be no corruption and where there is no iniquity the fruit of iniquity cannot be found.

Heaven is a sinless heaven. Corruption cannot enter or work there.

III. ITS PURITY - 'UNDEFILED'

Rev. 21:27 The redeemed of the Lord shall reside and walk there.

IV. ITS ETERNITY - 'THAT FADETH NOT AWAY'

There is an eternal permanence about heaven. It is the city which has foundations whose builder and maker is God. Its construction bears the marks of the Everlasting God. It is eternally gold stamped.

V. ITS SECURITY - 'RESERVED IN HEAVEN'

There is no doubt about this inheritance. It is secure. "FIRM as His throne His promise stands."

The inheritance is secured for you, 'reserved in heaven', and you are reserved for heaven, 'you - who are kept by the power of God unto salvation'. Heaven is most certainly a prepared place for a prepared people.

Heaven is the perfection of all perfections and the reapings of sin are all banished forever from heaven.

There are seven things which cannot be and will not be in heaven. The Seven 'No Mores'

1. No more SEA (Revelation 21:1). Sea speaks of sin in its troubles, storms and separations.
2. No more CURSE (Rev. 22:3)
3. No more DEATH (Rev. 21:4)
4. No more SORROW (Rev. 21:4)
5. No more CRYING (Rev. 21:4)
6. No more PAIN (Rev. 21:4)
7. No more NIGHT (Rev. 22:5)

By stark contrast hell is the very opposite to heaven.

What is not in heaven is in hell in the darkest and most terrible way.

No more SEA in heaven. But the place of the final hell's torment is called THE LAKE OF FIRE.

No more CURSE in heaven. But the lake of fire is the place of the final and everlasting curse of God on sinners.

No more DEATH in heaven. But the eternal torments of the damned are called 'the second death'.

No more SORROW in heaven. But the eternal punishment of the lost is the place of continual 'gnashing of teeth'.

No more CRYING in heaven. But the finally damned are weeping and wailing forever.

No more PAIN in heaven. But the inhabitants of the lake of fire are tormented forever.

No more NIGHT in heaven. But the everlasting lost are in the blackness of darkness forever. Remember it is heaven with Christ but it is hell without Christ.

So much for the negatives. Let us turn to seven positives in heaven, some inferred from the negatives already mentioned and some stated in the most affirmative way:-

There we have the unfolding of the final harmony, the uncovering of the otherwise hidden mystery and the revelation of what is and has been concealed for all time.

Seven dazzling perfections shine forth. No human eye dare look upon them. Only the pure in heart can see God and the eternal things of God.

I. PERFECT REDEMPTION

If there be no curse and the curse is gone (Rev. 21:3) there can only be blessings abounding and astounding.

Sin fully dealt with has been removed forever. The awful curse is gone. The brandmarks on Christ's body of suffering attest the truth that:-

> Said Justice 'Man I feign know what you weigh?
> If weight, I spare you. If too light, I slay.
> Man leap'd the scale - it mounted - 'Oh my word'
> (Said Justice) 'less than nothing! Where's my sword?'
> Virtue was there and her small weight would try;
> The scale unsunk, till kicked the beam on high
> Mercy the whitest dove that ever flew
> From Calvary, fetch'd a twig of crimson hue.
> Aloft it sent the scale on t'other side:
> *Man smiled and Justice awed, 'I'm satisfied.'*

Perfect redemption indeed!

II. PERFECT RESIDENCE

'The throne of God and of the Lamb shall be in it.' Rev. 22:3

'Behold the tabernacle of God is with men, and He will dwell with them and they shall be His people and God Himself shall be with them and be their God.' Rev. 21:3

God and the Lamb, 'tis well;
I know that Source Divine,
Of joy and love no tongue can tell
And know that all is mine.

God and the Lamb shall there
The light and temple be
And radiant hosts forever share
The unveiled mystery.

The Lamb is there my soul!
There God Himself doth rest
In love divine, diffused through all -
With Him supremely blessed.

III. PERFECT RELATIONSHIP
'His servants shall serve Him' Rev. 22:3

We speak of its service of love
Of the robes which the glorified wear,
The Church of the first born above,
But what must it be to be there!

Tongue cannot describe the wonder of the service we will engage in, in the blest city of God.

In total love, in total perfection and in total joy we shall serve our glorious Lord. We will serve Him the way we would liked to have served Him on earth. Sin gone forever! Weakness gone forever! Inability gone forever!

Keep us, Lord, O keep us cleaving
To Thyself, and still believing,
Till the hour of our receiving
Promised joys in heaven.

> Then we shall be where we would be,
> Then we shall be what we should be,
> That which is not now, nor could be
> *Then shall be our own.*

IV. THE PERFECT RECOGNITION
'And they shall see His face' Rev. 22:4

> Oh, what a joyful meeting there,
> In robes of white arrayed!
> We'll all unite in praising Him
> Whose glories never fade.
> Him eye to eye we soon shall see,
> Our face like His shall shine;
> Oh, what a glorious company,
> *When saints and angels join.*

V. THE PERFECT RESEMBLANCE
'His name shall be in their foreheads' Rev. 22: 4

We will all bear His blessed brand mark and that will be the perfect resemblance of us all. We shall all have a common seal. This forehead seal is spoken of throughout the Book of Revelation.

The seal of God on the forehead was for preservation - Rev. 7:3.
The absence of the seal was the appointment to judgment - Rev. 9:4.
The substitution of the seal by the mark of the beast. Rev. 13:14.
The identification of the seal with its privileges Rev. 14:1.

What a common resemblance all heaven's citizens shall have, the sons and daughters of God the Father through His Son and by His Spirit.

VI. THE PERFECT REST
'And there shall be no night there; and they need no candle, neither light of the sun; for the Lord God giveth them light:' Rev. 22:5

Night will be redundant because heaven has no weariness, no weakness and no tiredness. Where the God, who never slumbers and sleeps, reigns, there is always perfect rest - the saints everlasting rest. We will all be restfully busy in heaven forever.

> When there we meet the Saviour
> And see Him face to face,
> And there behold His glory.
> So full of truth and grace,
> We then shall know our pathway
> Was ordered for the best.
> It was our Father's right way
> To everlasting rest.

VII. THE PERFECT REIGN
"They shall reign forever and ever" Revelation 22:5

> The God who rules on high,
> Whose thunder rends the clouds,
> Who rides upon the stormy sky,
> And calms the raging floods -
>
> This holy God is ours,
> Encircling us with love.
> He shall put forth His mighty power
> To carry us above.
>
> There shall we see His face
> And never, never sin,
> And from the rivers of His grace
> Drink endless pleasures in.

It would be a worthwhile study for you to compare these seven characteristics of heaven with the seven promises to the overcomers in the seven churches of Asia. You will find a blessed parallelism and perfect order there.

When the Quaker John Greenleaf Whittier came to the end of his earthly pilgrimage, and as the earthly house of his bodily tabernacle was dissolving, he wrote a farewell poem in anticipation of heaven, and rightly called it "At Last".

> When on my day of life the night is falling,
> And, in the winds from unsunned spaces blown,
> I hear far voices out of darkness calling
> *My feet to paths unknown.*
>
> Thou who hast made my home of life so pleasant,
> Leave not its tenant when its walls decay;
> O Love Divine, O Helper ever present,
> Be Thou my strength and stay!
>
> Be near me when all else is from me drifting:
> Earth, sky, home's pictures, days of shade and shine,
> And kindly faces to my own uplifting
> The love which answers mine.
>
> I have but Thee, my Father! let Thy spirit
> Be with me then to comfort and uphold;
> No gate of pearl, no branch of palm I merit,
> Nor street of shining gold.
>
> Suffice it if - my good and ill unreckoned,
> And both forgiven through Thy abounding grace -
> I find myself by hands familiar beckoned
> Unto my fitting place.
>
> Some sweet door among Thy many mansions,
> Some sheltering shade where sin and striving cease,
> And flows for ever through heaven's green expansions
> The river of Thy peace.

There, from the music round about me stealing.
I fain would learn the new and holy song,
And find at last, beneath Thy trees of healing,
The life for which I long.

I conclude this series with a great sermon by the famous American Presbyterian preacher Theodore L Cuyler DD, who ministered for some 60 years in the gospel.

AN EYE ON HEAVEN

A wise man who is setting out for a foreign country - especially if he intends to reside there - will study the localities in that land, and seek to become acquainted with the language and the customs of its people. His thoughts will be much upon it. But do the great majority even of true Christians spend much time on thought about heaven? Yet it is to be their dwelling-place through innumerable ages. At no distant day - perhaps within a few days to some of us - the veil that hides the eternal world may drop, and the gates of the Father's house may open before our astonished vision! If heaven is ready for Christ's redeemed people, then surely they should be making ready for heaven.

THINK OFTEN ABOUT HEAVEN

We ought to be thinking more about our future and everlasting home. If our treasures are there, then our hearts should be there also in frequent and joyful anticipations. John Bunyan tells of his Pilgrim that "his heart waxed warm about the place whither he was going." This world is not our rest. It is only our temporary lodging-place, our battle ground to fight sin and Satan, our vineyard in which to labour for our Master and our fellow men until sundown and our training school for the development of character and growth in grace.

A thoroughly spiritual person, who makes Jesus Christ real and the powers of the world to become real, and who has set his affections on things above, must inevitably have some deep meditations about his home and his magnificent inheritance. He loves to read about it, and gathers up eagerly the few grand, striking things which his Bible tells him about the jasper walls, and the gates of pearl, and the trees that bear twelve manner of fruits, and the crystal streams that flow flashing from beneath the throne of God. Among his favourite hymns are "Jerusalem the Golden" and the "Shining Shore"; they are like rehearsals for his part by-and-by in the sublime oratorios of heaven. Sometimes, when cares press heavily, or bodily pains wax sharp, or bereavements darken his house, he gets homesick, and says, "Oh that I had wings like a dove; then would I fly away and be at rest."

MEDITATION OF HEAVEN HELPS US TO WORK HARDER ON EARTH

Such devout meditations do not prove any man or woman to be a dreamy mystic. They are not the pious sentimentalisings of mourners to whom this world has lost all its charm, or of enthusiasts whose religion evaporates in mere emotion.

The hundred-handed **Paul** constantly reminds his fellow workers that their "citizenship is in heaven".

The godly **Samuel Rutherford**, who was said to be always studying, always preaching, and always visiting the sick, found time to feed on anticipations of Paradise. He tells us that he often longed to "stand at the outer side of the gates of the New Jerusalem and look through a crevice of the door and see Christ's face." He exclaims, "O time, run fast! O fair day, when wilt thou dawn? O shadows flee away! O well-beloved Bridegroom, be Thou to me like the roe or the young hart of the mountains!"

No man in modern times had written any volume so full of heavenly aspirations as **Richard Baxter's** "Saint's Everlasting Rest". Yet Baxter was one of the most practical of philanthropists. While meditating on the Better Country he wore his busy life out in striving to make England a better country, and the town of Kidderminster was revolutionised by his ceaseless labours for the bodies and the souls of its inhabitants.

Intense spirituality and intense practicality were beautifully united in the late **Dr AJ Gordon** of Boston. If he kept one eye on heaven, he kept the other wide open to see the sins and the snares and the sorrows of his fellow creatures all around him. I verily believe that if we thought more about heaven, and realised more its ineffable blessedness, we would strive harder to get others there.

WE NEED TO HAVE THE HEAVENLY VISION

It is no wonder that some professed Christians do not catch more distinct glimpses of the celestial world. Their vision is obscured. A very small object when held close to the eye will hide even the sun at noonday, so a Christian may hold a dollar so close to the eye of his soul as to shut out both Christ and heaven. Fishes down in mammoth Cave become eyeless at last; and so will any of us lose even the faculty of seeing if we shut ourselves in a cavern of grinding worldliness or utter unbelief.

Perhaps some reader of this article may despondingly say, "Well, I never get any sight of heaven; I am all in a mist; nothing but clouds and darkness before my eyes." My friend, look where you are standing. You are in Satan's marshy grounds and among the quagmires where the fogs dwell continually. Ever since you left the "King's highway", ever since you forsook the straight path of duty, ever since you quit honest praying and Christian work, and God's Book for your ledger, and the service of Christ for the service of Mammon, you have strayed away into the devil's territory!

Heaven is not visible to backsliders. And never until your feet take hold again of that straight path of sincere, unselfish obedience to Jesus Christ, and your eyes are washed out with some sincere tears of repentance, will you have any fresh, gladdening glimpse of that rest which remaineth for the people of God. Throw off your load, my friend, and the sins that so easily beset you, and, getting your feet again in the track, run with patience the race set before you, looking unto Jesus.

THE JOY OF CONTEMPLATING HEAVEN

Those whose conversation is in heaven, and who keep it constantly before them, have abundant sources of spiritual joy, They renew their strength as they push upward and heavenward. What is it to them that the road is long and sometimes the hills of difficulty are steep, that there are often lions in the way, that there are crosses to be carried, that there are some valleys of death-shadow to be threaded, and that not far ahead is that river over which there is no bridge!

All these things do not disturb them. Heaven lieth at the end of the way, clothed in its purpose and its golden light. The mount Zion is there - the city of the living God and the innumerable company of angels, some of whom may turn out to be the old friends who have had their eye on us ever since we were born into Christ.

From the hilltops we can, with the spyglass of faith, bring heaven so near that we can see its "bulwarks with salvation strong" and "its streets of shining gold".

QUICKENED ZEAL

These views of the certain and assuredly promised inheritance of glory ought to quicken our zeal prodigiously. The time is short and shortening every day. If we are to have treasures there we must be securing them; no time is to be lost. If we are to lead any souls there we must be out after them. If we are to wear any crown there, however humble, we must win it. Christian zeal depends upon inward warmth; and much of that heat must come from heaven.

"When," exclaimed grand old Baxter, "When, O my soul, hast thou been warmest? When hast thou most forgot thy wintry sorrows? Is it not when thou hast got above, closest to Jesus Christ, and hast conversed with Him, and viewed the mansions of glory, and filled thyself with sweet foretastes and talked with the inhabitants of the higher world?"

Certain it is that he who loves not Christ and His fellow men loves not heaven; and he who loves not heaven is not very likely to see heaven.

A true life is just a tarrying and a toiling in this earthly tent for Christ until we go into the mansions with Christ.

Grow old along with me in Christ and each day will bring you nearer to being with Christ when we will never grow old any more.

APPENDIX ONE

THE FOUR WINDOWS OF LIFE
- A SKETCH OF MY LIFE STORY -

TWO SERMONS PREACHED BY DR. PAISLEY IN THE MARTRYS MEMORIAL FREE PRESBYTERIAN CHURCH ON THE THIRTY-SEVENTH ANNIVERSARY OF HIS MINISTRY

> "Get thee up into the top of Pisgah, and lift up thine eyes westward, and northward, and southward, and eastward, and behold it with thine eyes." Deuteronomy 3:27.

As I have announced, I want to preach both this morning and this evening on the subject, "The four windows through which I looked out into the world."

The Bible has much to say about windows. The first time the window is mentioned in the Bible is in Genesis chapter six. It is mentioned in relationship to the ark. Noah was ordered to make one window in the top of the ark - the window in the ark looked heavenward.

Then as we proceed to read in Genesis we find that Isaac's lie concerning his wife Rebekah was discovered by the king of Gera as he looked through the window.

When we come to the Book of Joshua we have the window with the scarlet thread - the window of the sign of redemption.

In the Book of Judges we find that the mother of Sisera looked out through the window expecting her son to come home triumphantly, but instead of triumph there was defeat - the window of false hope.

In the first Book of Samuel we have David escaping, through the window, with the help of his wife Michal, the daughter of king Saul. That has a parallel in the New Testament when Paul tells us he was lowered in a basket through the window from his enemies in the city of Damascus - the window of deliverance.

In Solomon's Song we discover the window of the unveiling of the bridegroom. He showed himself at the window.

We then have the window of testimony in the life of Daniel. He opened the windows of his room towards Jerusalem and he prayed, defying the commandment of the king. This resulted in his being cast into the den of lions.

We also read in the Book of the Acts of a young man who went to sleep in the window. As a result he fell out through the window. (Don't you be doing that this morning!) The apostle Paul gave him the resurrection touch and the window of sleep became the window of resurrection.

That will happen to us all. The window of the sleep of death, if the Lord tarries, will also become the window of resurrection. The body of the believer is not buried, the body of the believer is sown, and when you sow something you look for a harvest. There will be a glorious harvest - the glorious resurrection of the bodies of all believers.

There is too, the window of scorn. When Michal, the wife of David, looked through the window and despised her husband she brought judgment upon herself.

Finally the window of the vision of destruction. In Proverbs, the wise man looked through the window and he saw the pilgrimage of the fool to the place of destruction and to the pit of Hell itself.

I want now to refer you to the text which I have just read. This text in Deuteronomy chapter three, has four windows. It has a window westward, it has a window northward, it has a window southward and it has a window eastward. I want to start at the end of the text, because there is a Spiritual principle that the last shall be first, and the first shall be last. So we have an eastward window, then we have a southward window, then we have a northward window, and then we have a westward window. That, of course, is the right order for us.

One: The Eastward Window - The Window Of Our Childhood.

The sun rises in the east, so the first window is the window of our childhood, when the sun rises and we look out on the promised land of life.

Two: The Southward Window - The Window Of Our Youth.

We come to the window that is south and we are looking directly towards the sun, and that speaks to us of the window of our youth.

Three: The Northward Window - The Window Of Maturity.

We come to the north, with its hard clear light speaking to us of the window of maturity.

Four: The Westward Window - The Window Of The Sun Setting - The Window Of Declining Years.

We come to the west window, the sun-setting and that speaks to us of the window of declining years.

I want to take a look out of the windows that are east and south this morning, then we will look out of the north and west this evening.

ONE: THE EAST WINDOW OF CHILDHOOD

The east window of childhood. A child has a wonderful experience, because the child takes the first look out of the window, and it is sunrise on the promised land.

I don't know what you recollect about your childhood, but I recollect three very important things.

The first thing is my conversion to Christ. I will never forget that.

The second thing is the power of evangelistic preaching.

The third thing is the value of the human soul.

THE FIRST THING I REMEMBER IS MY CONVERSION

The twenty-ninth day of May, nineteen hundred and thirty-two, is my spiritual birthday. I will never forget that day. My mother, who is now in the Glory Land, preached from this Bible. I'm glad I have this Bible. It is a treasure. It is stained with mother's tears and it is marked by mother's fingerprints.

The text was John 10:11: "I am the Good Shepherd, the Good Shepherd giveth His life for the sheep." After my mother was laid to rest I was going through her papers and I found the notes of that little sermon which she preached that day. Yes, and that day, as a boy of six, I came to Jesus as I was. I found in Him a resting place, and Hallelujah, He did make me glad. Conversion! It is a wonderful thing to look out of the window and discover the Way to Heaven. Thank God, I found that Way through God's Lamb, sacrificed for me.

THE SECOND THING I RECOLLECT ABOUT CHILDHOOD IS THE PICTURE I HAVE HERE, THE PICTURE OF GENERAL BOOTH, THE FOUNDER OF THE SALVATION ARMY

It hung above my bed (this is a replica of the actual picture, kindly sent to me by the present General of the Salvation Army when I told him that I used to have the picture hanging above my bed.) Every night, after I said my prayers, I used to look at the old General and say, "I want to pray and preach like him." That is why I have the text *Salvation to the uttermost"* on the wall of this church, for that is the text which imprinted itself on my mind as a child. As a boy I looked out of that east window and I got a vision of the power of prayer and the power of the preaching of God's Word. Those are things which never can be erased, those first things from the window of childhood.

THE THIRD THING THAT WILL NEVER BE ERASED FROM MY CHILDISH RECOLLECTION IS THE VALUE OF A HUMAN SOUL

It was my great privilege as a child to meet the honoured servants of God who came to our home and who preached for my dad. I'm thinking now of one of them, Evangelist Tom Rea. I remember the church packed to capacity. I remember that eminent servant standing up and preaching, and as he preached I heard big men sob. I saw and heard one man cry out and say, "Preacher, I'll get saved now." Those were old-time converting meetings. Sadly, we don't have them today. That was a time when the power of God fell upon the preacher as he preached the Word. Now those old-time preachers, by the standards of modern homiletics and etiquette, broke every rule in the book, but they broke the hearts of their hearers in preaching God's Truth with power.

I can never forget as I looked through the east window and got the vision of the promised land. It was a land where one needed the conversion of the Spirit of God in the new birth. It was a land that could only be trodden by the foot of prayer and the promises of God. It was a land that was enriched by the fruit of the ministry of the Word in the salvation of precious souls.

TWO: THE SOUTH WINDOW OF YOUTH

Childhood passes very quickly and we soon come to that window that is south - the window of youth. As I looked through the south window I discovered that something had happened to me, I had become a preacher. I preached my first sermon. It was not a long sermon, it lasted about four to five minutes. It was however the beginning of my preaching ministry. I will never forget the text which I used. It was about the man going down from Jerusalem to Jericho. I tell you, after I preached that sermon I felt like that man. I had fallen among thieves and someone had stolen all my thoughts and words. I was confident that I could have preached for half an hour but four minutes exhausted me. I will never forget it. That was looking out through the window of youth. It was an important Sabbath Day for me. I was just fifteen years of age, entering shortly into my sixteenth year, and I started my preaching ministry.

PREACHING IN THE WELSH VALLEYS

That same year I travelled over to South Wales and enrolled in what is now the South Wales Bible College, but was then known as the Barry School of Evangelism. I studied under an old revival preacher of the 1904 Welsh Revival, the Rev B S Fiddler. It was the middle of World War II. I enlisted, immediately I arrived, in the Civil Defence Corps of that town of Barry. I was out on duty during one of the great German air raids which struck Cardiff. I will never forget that night. It is impressed in my memory. I saw the German bombers come in and I saw the bombs dropping, and the flames going up. I witnessed one of those bombers shot down into the sea.

I was reminded, as I took a look through that south window, that sin was sin, that evil was evil, that there was a devil abroad in the land, and that it behoved me to remember that I had only one life, it would soon be past, and that only what was done for Jesus Christ would last.

I commenced to practise preaching upon the long-suffering congregations in the Welsh valleys.

I AM A DEBTOR

I owe a lot to Wales. I owe a lot to those little chapels, as they called them, spotted over the valleys. I would set out every Sabbath morning on a bicycle, ride many miles, come to a little church nestled in the hillside or in a small village, go in and wait until the people gathered, mount the pulpit, give out the hymns, pray and preach. I didn't have any difficulty, I could preach for an hour and it came more easily to me. Some congregations received me graciously, other congregations didn't receive me graciously. I was an Ulsterman and lacked the richness of the wonderful Welsh tongue.

I remember travelling something like fifteen miles one Sunday morning to preach in a certain church. When I arrived one of the deacons met me and he said, "We didn't expect you until this evening. We were not going to have a preacher today, so few people come to the morning service. Seeing you are here however we will allow you to preach." So I preached that sermon and it must have been a very poor sermon, because after I had finished, the same deacon came to me and he said, "We cannot give you any dinner, you will have to cycle back to Barry." That meant another fifteen miles back to the College. I tell you, I got my own back that night on that congregation, and I'm sure they would remember the fiery Ulsterman who reminded them of their lack of hospitality in the morning. In fact when I told my dad about that, he said, "Son, you should have done what another preacher did. He was not given his lunch by the congregation, so the next Sunday when he came back to preach he had his lunch tied up in a large cloth, which he hung over the light by the side of the pulpit. Then every time he wanted to impress his congregation he would say, 'As sure as my lunch is in that handkerchief, so sure if you sinners are not converted you will be in Hell.' I tell you, they never asked him to bring his lunch again. He had offers from about ten members to come for lunch on the following Sunday."

I'm afraid I didn't get those offers, but if I had been as wise as that old preacher I might have done.

TOO YOUNG TO PREACH!

The Rev BS Fiddler was a great revival preacher. Some of the largest congregations in Wales were always booking him for great services. I remember one Sunday afternoon - I'll never forget it - the Principal's wife came to my room and she said, "The Principal wants to see you." I went down. He was in bed very ill. He said to me, "Paisley, I can't go to preach this evening. You will have to go, it is one of the best attended churches in Wales. You will have a congregation of at least 500 people." That to me in those days was more like 5,000, and I was terrified. He said, "You have to ride about 15 miles, so you better get started."

I rode away to this place in one of the valleys, and when I got about a mile from the church I had a flat tyre, so I had to walk the last mile or so to the service. When I got near to the church all I could see were these crowds of people pouring into the building. As I entered one of the deacons who was standing there said, "Who are you?" I said, "I am the preacher." "What? A boy like you!" I said, "Yes, Mr Fiddler is ill, I'm his substitute." He said, "Can he not get anybody better than you?" I said, "I'm afraid not." "Well," he said, "We have no one else so we will have to trust you."

I remember going out into that church, and, of course, the 500 people in that church looked, as I said, more like 5,000 to this preacher of some sixteen years of age. I remember standing up and giving out the first hymn and praying for spiritual power. God was good to the preacher. I preached upon that text, "Thou fool, this night thy soul shall be required of thee." When I had finished my preaching, (they always have an after meeting in the Welsh churches resulting from the great 1904 revival), that old deacon got up and said, "I was very disappointed when this young stripling came to our church tonight, but, no doubt, the hand of God is upon him and we have heard the Word of God preached this night with power." I trust that on the great Judgment Day some soul from that meeting will meet me at God's right hand, and then my Heaven will be two Heavens in Emmanuel's Land!

Those were the days when I looked through the south window.

ORDAINED AND PLACED

I returned home, and entered the Theological Hall of the Reformed Presbyterian Church of Ireland. For a further three years I studied and prepared myself for the ministry. That brings me to 1st August, 1946, when I was ordained as a minister of Christ on this road. I never will forget that service. There are two people in our congregation this morning who were present then, and I am the third. What a toll thirty seven years takes! The Rev WJ Grier BA, the minister of Stranmillis Evangelical Presbyterian Church, who passed on to be with the Lord just this past week, preached the ordination sermon. He exhorted me to be strong in the Lord and in the power of the might of God, to contend earnestly for the faith, to stand true to the principles of the Bible in a day of apostasy, declension and evil. I remember one quotation he made, I will never forget it. He said, "Let me quote to you, young man, the words of Samuel Rutherford the great Covenanting preacher, 'Give not one hair's breadth of God's truth away, for it is not yours to give, it is God's.'" Give not one hair's breadth of God's truth away! While men are giving away God's truth wholesale today I have sought not to give one hair's breadth of God's truth away.

My dad gave me the ordination charge. I remember him saying to me, "Son, desire to receive in your soul the touch of the nail-pierced hand. Let yours be the mighty ordination of the Son of God." I remember him turning to that great charge to young Timothy, and with his heart filled with love for his boy he charged me before God and the Lord Jesus, to preach the Word, to be instant in season, out of season, to reprove, rebuke, exhort, with longsuffering and godliness, for the time would come when they would not endure sound doctrine." Truly that time has come.

The Rev Thomas Rowan MA, an Irish Presbyterian minister, who was an associate of DL Moody in Moody's later years, brought the charge to the congregation. Then godly men laid their hands upon me and set me aside for the preaching of the Blessed Word of God.

AN UNFORGETTABLE PRAYER

Thirty-seven years is a long time, yet the freshness of that ordination service is with me today. There is one thing which is still with me, and that is the prayer that was offered by one of my professors in the Theological Hall of the Reformed Presbyterian Church, Professor TB McFarland BA of Newry. I can see now in memory that old man lift his hands and pray. Ah! with what power he prayed, praying that God's strength and grace and help would be given to the young man ordained; that he should be kept faithful and true; that his ministry might have upon it the blessing and benediction of Heaven, and that the power of God might be seen in the conversion of precious souls.

The following Lord's Day I preached my first two sermons as the minister of the congregation here. I remember the text, "I am determined to know nothing among you save Jesus Christ and Him crucified." When I entered the church that morning, who was sitting in the back seat but the Rev WP Nicholson. If I was terrified before I entered the service, I was more terrified then. But I preached. After I had finished Mr Nicholson got up, walked forward to the Communion Table, rapped it, and said to me:

A TONGUE LIKE AN OLD COW

"Young man, have you ever seen a cow's tongue?" I said, "Yes, sir." He said, "What is it like?" I said, "It is like a file." Then he lifted his hands and prayed, "Lord, give this young man a tongue like an old cow," I'll never forget that prayer. I met the great preacher afterwards and I said to him "Your prayer is being answered, for some of the enemies of the Gospel are feeling the file of the preacher's words."

I was just then turned twenty years of age, a mere stripling, but I took my look out of the south window.

THREE: THE NORTH WINDOW OF MATURITY

We now come to the northward look. North speaks to us of the strong clearness of the sun looking towards the north. It is crisp. The air is clear. The day is full. The vision is complete.

Let me remind you that each window, each look, was towards the promised land.

As a child I looked towards the promised land, and, thank God, I found the Saviour and started to go in the pilgrim path to that land that is fairer than day.

In youth I saw the promised land and prepared myself for the ministry of the Gospel, to take others with me to the promised land.

I want to come to that wonderful northward window. You know, to the child everything is wonderful. There are no difficulties. A child doesn't see any difficulties, everything can be done, and if he can't do it his dad can do it, and if his dad can't do it there is one sure thing, mummy can do it. There is no doubt about that. That is the child's attitude.

Then to youth everything is challenging, interesting, inviting, beckoning. When, however, we look out of the north window in maturity we get a glimpse of reality. We learn that there are things which are not for us. You know, the greatest thing in life is contentment. Do you know that? Just to be content with your lot. Some people are never content. (Of course to us men it is easier to be content, but for them, bless their little hearts, it is a real difficulty for a woman to be content). But contentment with godliness is great gain.

I have taken a look out of the north window and I have learned something, "Seekest thou great things for thyself, seek them not." You needn't worry about the future, for God has planned it. If you walk in His will He will open every door that needs to be opened, and every door that should not be opened will be bolted and locked and you will not get through that door anyway, so there is no use in hammering upon it. What a wonderful thing it is to know that our lives are planned by the Heavenly Father.

> He know, He loves, He cares.
> Nothing His Truth can dim.
> He does the very best for those
> Who leave the choice with Him.

OLD RAVENHILL

When I came to this Road I threw myself into the work. I had a small church, which is still standing, down the road, (now our Church Hall). We had 346 seats, I counted every one of them, and I had a congregation of sixty. Sixty people signed the call that brought me to this road, and there were children as well as adults. I preached for six months and I preached the most moving sermons of my life, because half the congregation left. Then I said, "Ian, if you are going to stay on this road you had better get people into church."' So I went on the door knockers. One morning at nine o'clock I went round the corner. I started in a good street, Shamrock Street, and I knocked my first door. A little lady opened the door and looked at me. I said as politely as I could in good broad Ballymena brogue, "Good morning." She said, "Good morning." Then she looked me up and down and she snapped, "Are you the young preacher from round the corner?" I smiled graciously and said, "I am." She said, "God Almighty help you amongst that bunch!" She slammed the door, and there I was standing on the doorstep.

I made a vow that no one would ever slam a door on me again. So when I went to the next house I put my big foot through the door and many a person struggled to close the door, but that foot kept it open and many a time I preached through the little slot as they attempted to close the door. I was zealous for the work of the Lord.

THE PROTESTANT CONTROVERSY

There was a great battle on in this Province at that time for the Protestant cause. My uncle had been appointed in London as the General Secretary of the National Union of Protestants. I was the first paid officer of that Union in Northern Ireland. We had great rallies both in the Ulster Hall and in the Wellington Hall. The great battle was on the State School issue versus the Roman Catholic School. At that time the Unionist Government wanted to increase the grants to the Roman Catholic Schools. So I was thrown, in my early ministry, into the Protestant controversy. I have never regretted that and never will, for from my head to my toe I am a Protestant, and if there is any dirt under the toenails it is Protestant dirt, I can however assure you there is none for I bathed this morning!

EVANGELISM

I had a spirit of evangelism. Dear brother John Costley who is sitting here tonight, and I am glad he is with us, I trust the Lord will keep him with us for a long time, said to me, "Would you like to preach an evangelistic mission? Being a young preacher I said, "Certainly." He said "there is a little Mission Hall in Keswick Street on the Shankill Road. It was a spirit grocer's. The Christians have bought it over. They have turned the counter into a little preaching desk. It holds about 50 people, but you could have a good campaign."

So I went to Keswick Street and I had a great evangelistic campaign, and many souls were saved. One of the first souls in that Mission was a Miss Hazel Miskimmon who became a missionary for the Acre Gospel Mission in Brazil, and she is still serving on that mission field. So I tasted the thrill of evangelism.

Nevertheless, with all my preaching, with all my contending, I felt there was a lack of power. I needed an anointing, I needed holy fire, I needed power in the pulpit work of the Church.

MY FIRST NIGHT OF PRAYER

Rev William P Nicholson came at that time to this city and I attended an all night of prayer, the first all night of prayer I had ever attended. I have attended hundreds of them since. It was in the old CWU Hall in Donegall Pass. The hall was packed with men, I will never forget it. Mr Nicholson sat at a table in the middle of the room, and he made remarks about everybody who prayed. There was one man who prayed in a very high pitched voice, and I remember WP saying, "You must have been a beautiful baby, you must have been a beautiful child." I laughed more at that prayer meeting than I prayed, but I discovered something, that prayer was to be enjoyed. There are some people and when they get to a prayer meeting they think it is a Protestant "purgatory", I believe that prayer meetings should be the thrill of your heart and your soul. So I learned the blessing of praying all night.

THE ANOINTING

In October 1949 I said to three men, brother John Douglas, now the Rev John Douglas and the principal of Whitefield College of the Bible, brother Robert Scott who became a missionary to India and is now living and working for the Lord in the United States of America, and brother Welsh who is still with us in our congregation, "Let us have a night of prayer." So about ten o'clock the four of us met. Little did we know what was going to happen at that prayer meeting. We prayed on until about one o'clock. John Douglas was only a lad at the time. He said, "I had better go home, my mother will wonder what has happened to me." So he went home and we prayed on, and two o'clock, three o'clock, four o'clock, five o'clock, six o'clock came and the sun rose and it found us still on our knees. We went on praying. We couldn't leave the house. We prayed all that day.

I remember brother Welsh (he wasn't married at the time, and was lodging with a member of this church) leaving and going to his digs. He there discovered that his landlady had been baking a cake. So he opened the oven and he brought this fresh cake down to us. I remember Bob Scott and me breaking that cake, eating it and saying, "Thank God, may it be like the morsel that Elijah had when he was able to go forty days and forty nights on the angel's cooking." We prayed on.

Night came and were still in prayer, and then suddenly God gave us a sweet and blessed assurance that He had anointed us with power. We didn't have any charismatic itch. We didn't have any tongues experience. We didn't have anything of that nature whatsoever but we had a peace as calm as a river, a peace that the friends of this world never knew. I jumped to my feet, and said, "Glory to God, the anointing of God is upon me, I wish it were the Sabbath." We didn't have long to wait. Sabbath Day came. I didn't go into the pulpit. I stood at the Communion Table, and I preached on the subject "Three altars, at which one will you bow?" The altar of normal Christian experience, the altar of worldliness, or the altar of complete dedication to Christ? There was a little man in the church. He had always been critical of my ministry, and as I preached he said right out "He is mad", and he left. Well, that was a seat for some other sinner to come and occupy.

That evening God came down our souls to greet, and the first person that was saved in that movement of the Spirit was Bob Scott's mother. She came to Christ that night. Ever since that night there has not been a week that God has not saved souls on this road. If they weren't saved on Sunday night they came to the Manse. If they weren't saved in the Manse they phoned me and I went to see them, but ever since God has been saving souls on the Ravenhill Road. It has nothing to do with me, praise God it has to do with the gracious anointing of the Spirit of God. To God be the glory! Of course, I am a nobody and a nothing, and everybody will tell you that. They will say that I'm only an upstart. Glorious upstart for the Lord! I have caused a lot of trouble to the Devil's crowd. I intend to cause a lot more trouble before I'm through with my ministry. The Lord has done it.

THE DEVIL IN A SKIRT

Well, if my preaching lacked fire it now caught fire, but I tell you when that happens in a church you are in for trouble, and I was sure in for trouble. When you meet the Devil in trousers he is very vicious, but when you meet the Devil in a skirt, then you are for it! I met the Devil in a skirt. There was one woman in that congregation and she vowed that she would finish me for good.

Of course that sort of thing has to come to a head and it came to a head one night when I preached a sermon on Hell. Her unconverted father was in the meeting and she was very upset that I would dare to talk about Hell and offend her father. Going out she said to me, "I want to talk with you." I said, "All right, in fact I would like to talk with you." So we went into the little room and we shut the door and she started on me. She said, "Your ministry is finished here." I said, "I'm glad to know it. I would like to get away, there are wider places than this, but I can't get away for the

Lord has told me I'm going to be around here for a very long time." She said, "You are mistaken, my husband is on the Church Committee, my father-in-law is an elder. We control this church, and young man, you are going."

I said, "Isn't that strange, because I wanted to tell you for a long time that you were going. Now tomorrow night the elders will meet, and the trustees will meet, and they will make a decision, and it will be very simple. They will either say, 'Preacher, you stay,' or they will say to you 'Go'." She said, "Right".

So the night came and I walked into that church. I had perfect peace. I wasn't afraid of losing a pulpit, for if I hadn't that pulpit I would have preached on the Ravenhill Road. It would not have made any difference to me. We might have had this church built 20 years before it was. I walked in, and she had her armour on. The greatest weapon a woman has is tears, and she was there weeping. She said, "Oh, Mr Paisley, do we need to have this meeting?" I said, "We certainly do, and either you are going or I am going." She said, "Could we not come to an agreement?" I said, "I'm sorry. You know what you have done? You have criticised every person I have led to the Lord in this church, and I want to tell you, the little ones will be offended no more. It is now or never." I walked into that room and I said to the elders, "Gentlemen, I'm just a boy, a stripling, but I believe the Book, and I want to tell you men, I'm going to preach this Book. I'll either preach it in here or out there. Make a choice, I don't want to be hard, I don't want to be cruel but this woman has to go." I left, and in a few minutes I was recalled, and they said "She has gone, and you are to stay." I said, "Gentlemen, you have made the right decision, let us get down to prayer."

Of course, she didn't go on her own, she visited every member of the congregation, she took a lot of people with her. There was I with more empty seats. So I decided that instead of having a prayer meeting, we would have a night of prayer every week and we would pray on the seats that nobody sat in. We went up into the little gallery and you could have written on the dust that had accumulated on those empty seats and we prayed at every one of them. It was a dusty prayer meeting I can assure you, but as we prayed at every seat, things started to move. Then, of course, the Lord opened doors.

RATHFRILAND

I went to Rathfriland and I started a Mission in the Friends' Hall. The first week it could not contain the people and we moved to the First Presbyterian Church Hall. (I was a good boy in those days, I wasn't the bad fellow I am tonight), and it was too small. We moved into the First Presbyterian Church and God saved something like 180 souls, and what a time we had! That is the first time I met brother George McKnight. He became an elder in our Moneyslane Church and has just died.

ORANGE HALL

We moved on to Drumlough. I then held a Mission in the YMCA at Mountpottinger, and my colleagues in that Mission, strange to relate, were the Rev Ivor Lewis and the Rev Donald Gillies. I was looking at an advertisement of that Mission recently.

I came back to my own Church and the trouble was still on - trouble over song leaders, so I decided that I would become a songleader. By the way, I had a choir in those days, but I sacked the choir, and I told the congregation to sing, "No, not one! No, not one!" We have never had a choir again except on Children's Day, because the choir, Mr Nicholson told me, was the war department of the church and you were better without it.

CROSSGAR

Let me say, I went for campaigns to Lisburn and Ballymena. One of my best campaigns was in Ballymena when I had nearly 500 souls. Then I was invited to Crossgar in 1951. I went down on the Saturday night. We were having a march, and the Boys Brigade from Lissara Presbyterian Church, was to lead the parade. Earlier that day the Presbytery of Down met and decided that they wouldn't grant us the use of the hall. So we came face to face with opposition to the Gospel. We went to the Killyleagh Street Hall. We had our Mission, and a gracious move of the Holy Spirit. The people who were saved and the people who had fought for the use of their own church for the preaching of the Gospel and had it denied by the Presbytery of Down, said to me, "Ian, we cannot stay in a church that has shut out the Gospel." So we had another day of prayer, and we decided that the time had come when we must challenge the great apostasy of our day.

OSTRACISED

If I had known what was going to happen I confess I would have taken fright and run away. At that time when I preached I had large services. I was well received by all denominations. I was preaching to crowds. God had blessed my ministry. But the day that I took a stand against the World Council of Churches and apostasy in the great denominations and in the Irish Presbyterian Church, my congregations disappeared. Instead of preaching to hundreds I preached to dozens. Instead of preaching and seeing scores saved, I saw one or two. I said, "Lord, why is it?" The Lord said to me, "It is none of your business. You just be faithful. If I want you to preach in a tin hut with ten people that is My business. If I want you to preach to crowds, that is My business, so you keep faithful."

So I kept faithful. We had problems with new congregations. We had problems across this country, and Ian Paisley was looked upon as a devil with horns, hoofs, and tail, but through good report and ill report I battled on, and I am still, Hallelujah, battling today.

One thing I really regret, I am fatter today than I was then. I wish I was the nice thin young fellow that I was in those days. But I battled on and God was good and merciful, and soon the tide started to rise, the blessing started to come, new congregations were formed, and all the time we were battling against resurgent Romanism and apostasy.

Then came that famous June, 1966, I will never forget that, and we walked to the General Assembly to make our protest, and we were met by "chronic squares" down at Cromac Square. The Pope's confetti greeted us and we were savagely attacked. Nevertheless we marched on and we made our protest. That was the day when a very important gentleman ruled supreme at Stormont House, Mr Terence O'Neill, now Lord O'Neill of the Maine.

The next day the then Moderator of the General Assembly, Dr. Alfie Martin, appeared at Stormont House. He had a close consultation with Mr Terence O'Neill and afterwards he came out and said he was glad to tell his brethren that the Prime Minister would deal with Ian Paisley and the Free Presbyterians. So we were dealt with. Many people who threw the missiles were not prosecuted, but we were prosecuted and brought to court.

JAILED

Now, of course, Mr Terence O'Neill had no intention of putting us in prison. He knew that that would be a wrong move, so he had the magistrates bind us over to keep the peace, thinking that we would stop our protests and be good boys for two years. My wife said to me, "He is a very foolish man, for I can't keep you quiet for five minutes and he wants to keep you quiet for two years." Rev John Wylie, Rev Ivan Foster and Ian Paisley said, "No surrender", and we meant it, so into the Crumlin Road Prison we went. It was the best thing that ever happened to us. For three months this Province was in a turmoil, people began to think about what was happening in the major denominations. Three Protestant preachers in prison!

My wife always was a preacher and preached well to me (and I was always receptive to her preaching), developed her gift and went round the country. She really gave it to Terence O'Neill. She said: "Terence O'Neill was cut out for a man but his mother lost the pattern." Of course, I would never say a thing like that, I'm too gracious to say such a thing! Anyway the imprisonment went on and I came out of prison. Do you know what happened the first Sunday I came out of prison? This hand received into membership over 200 new members who had been saved or had separated from apostasy during the time I was in prison. So you know what my elders said to me? They said, "If we get over 200 new members in the church for three months imprisonment, you should have stayed in for six." I said to them, "You can do the three other months, gentlemen, I'll just stay out now that I am out."

THE SPREAD OF THE WORK

The Free Church caught fire, and church after church was formed and the Lord blessed the ministry of His precious Word. To God be the glory! We are not only preaching the Gospel in Ulster, we have a flourishing congregation in the Irish Republic. We have a church now in Liverpool. We have one in Southern Australia. We have one in Toronto (I preached there last Monday night to a packed house, and what a time of blessing we had. We have a church in Calgary on the edge of the great

Rocky Mountain range, and we are soon going to have another church in Vancouver. We have a church in Pennsylvania and we have one in Greenville, and the best has yet to be and the end is not yet, praise the Lord!

It had nothing to do with me. It had all to do with the Lord. What God can do through the weakest weapon!

GOD'S LAUGH AT THE DEVIL

I'll tell you what it is, the Free Presbyterian Church is God's laugh at the Devil's crowd. You know God laughs, "He that sitteth in the heavens shall laugh." John the Baptist was God's laugh at the Pharisees. They had their schools. They had their Sanhedrin. They had Herod's temple. They had everything, but there was a fiery preacher, he was a Baptist, John the Baptist. We need a few more of them around today. We would be in good company if we had John the Baptist back again. We may not like his menu, locusts and wild honey - but no doubt we could enjoy the company of John the Baptist. He was God's laugh at the Pharisees and Sadducees. No wonder they were "sad you see". The early apostles Peter and John were called "unlearned and ignorant", but they had been with Jesus. That is all the Free Presbyterian Church is, just a lot of people who have been with Jesus. That is the secret of it all. People say, "When you die, Paisley, it will all die." I want to tell you it will be far greater after I go, because God will then be able to show that He is doing this work, and He will continue to do it until the end of the age.

A CLOWN FOR CHRIST

The fire of evangelism never burned low in my heart, I have an evangelistic heart. I remember walking up this road, (our Prayer Meeting was on Thursday night in those days), and I saw a big circus tent out there in the park, Rico's Circus tent. I said, "I would love to preach in that tent." So bold as brass I went to the tent and I said, "Where is Mr Rico?" A wee man came out and he said "I am Mr Rico." I said, "I am Ian Paisley." He said, "your reverence, what can I do for you?" I said, "I want to preach in your tent." He said, "That is interesting, because one of the English Bishops preached in that tent. So if he preached in it, it should be all right for you, sir. You can have it, and what is more, I'll announce that you are preaching here. I'll announce it at every circus performance this week."

So I got a free tent, free advertising, and I had a great meeting in that tent. My enemies said I was a clown anyway - well it is a good thing to be a fool for Jesus.

I have been a fool for Jesus. I stood down at the bottom of this Road, at a meeting of my young people at the park gates. A man came along, staggering under the influence of booze. (Never laugh at a drunk man. Shed tears for him, and thank God you were never in his place.) I went over to that man, put my arm around him, and said, "Sir, I've got good news for you." He said, "What do you mean? Nobody cares for me." I said, "Jesus loves you." He said, "Do you know who you are talking to? I went bail for my friend. He has skipped bail, the bailiffs have lifted everything I have. I'm going to throw myself into the River Lagan tonight. That is why I am drunk." I said, "No you are not going to throw yourself in the Lagan, you are going to meet the Lord Jesus tonight. Will you come down to the little church?" He said, "I would love to, but I couldn't make it. I'm full drunk." I said, "I can carry you." So I carried him down the Ravenhill Road, and as I passed by no doubt the onlookers said, "There is that fool Paisley." I got him into the old church. I used to ask him, "What happened then?" He said, "You carried me in and you put me into the little prayer room at the front of the church and you shut me in. You then went out into the outer building, and you prayed a prayer that sobered me for all time."

I said, "What did I say?" He said, "You said, 'O, God, You said that You answer prayer. Now, God I want You to save that man and sober him, and make him a testimony on this road, and if You don't do it I will never preach again!'" (That is real praying. When you get praying like that you are going places.) He said that that made him say to himself, "I am going to put this minister out of a job. I had better sober up." Then I went in and led him to the Lord. That was Saturday night!

WORRYING OVER A CONVERT

He was back on Sunday night. He said to me, "Preacher, I got saved last night, I was drunk, I'm going to get saved tonight, now that I'm sober." I am a Calvinist, but I wasn't going to argue with his theology, so I said, "Right". He went back into the room and he said, "Lord, I came to You last night and I was drunk, and You took me in, but I am just coming when I'm sober tonight to make sure about it," and he thanked God he had been saved. That man was Joe Black. He was my right-hand man for years on this Road. He worked in the Shipyard, a crane man. He never went home with a full pay packet from the Yard. Instead he went straight to the pub every Friday night, drunk most of his pay packet, and broke his wife's heart.

I worried about him the next Friday night. When I was a young preacher I was like the little boy who was given a tulip bulb. He planted it in his mother's garden, and he dug it up every day to see if it was growing! I was like that with young converts.

If a person is a Paisley convert he will go to Hell, if he is the Lord's convert he will be saved forever. The next Friday night, I worried about Joe, I prayed for him. On Sunday morning he was in his seat, I said, "He looks pretty sober, he must be all right, he must have made it." After I finished preaching I ran down from the pulpit, and I said, "Joe, what happened on Friday night?" He laughed and said, "you don't know. When I got my pay packet on Friday night I looked at it and said, 'Devil, you and booze robbed my wife of that pay packet for years, she is going to get it full tonight, but before she gets it I am gong to the pub and I'm going to stand in the door of that pub and have an open air meeting, I'm going to praise God I'm saved, and I'll never need to go in there any more.'" He then said, "I went to the pub, and the boys said, 'Are you coming in Joe?' I said, 'Never again', and I took off my old peaked cap and I screwed it up and held it in my hand and then I put my other hand into my pocket and said, 'Thank you Lord, I will never need to go in there and booze again.' Thank God I'm saved."

A LIFE SENTENCE

His companions said, "Joe, we will give you till next Friday." Next Friday came, Joe never was back in the pub. Then they said they would give him till the 12th of July, the 12th of July cane, he wasn't back in the pub. They said they would give him till the 12th August. The 12th August came, he wasn't back in the pub. Then they said they would give him till Black Saturday. Black Saturday came, he wasn't back in the pub. Then they said, "He will never make another Christmas." But he made it over that Christmas and every Christmas that came since. It was an Everlasting Life Sentence Joe got!

Tonight up yonder in the golden streets of Heaven Joe Black, my old friend, is singing the praises of Jesus, and I'm going to meet him and we are going to put our arms around one another and we are going to bless God for God's salvation.

There are men in this church tonight. You don't know them but when I came to this road they were drunkards and vagabonds and gamblers, and they walked on the dirty side of the road to Hell. Tonight they are clean and pure and for years they have worshipped God down in our old Church, in the Ulster Hall, and now in this house. Why? Because Jesus saved them. I believe Jesus saves, and His Blood washes whiter than snow!

FOUR: THE WEST WINDOW OF THE SUNSET

I'm getting old now, I tell my boys and girls that every day and they laugh at me. They say, "Daddy, you are just bluffing." No, I am not. Three more years I will be sixty. I'm getting old.

I have taken a look, my friend, through the west window. All the godly men who took part in my ordination service are now gone. My dad, the Rev Thomas Rowan, Professor TB McFarland, and now the Rev WJ Grier, they are all gone. I'm going too. There will be a day come when this pulpit will be empty. Ian Paisley will not be preaching here any more. There will be a day when I'll have finished my ministry. I hope that in Heaven I will be able to read what they said about me when I'm gone. I am told the Press have already written my Obituary Notice. I would love to have a look at it. I'm sure it is sweet, juicy and interesting. But let me tell you something, friend, when you read in the press that Ian Paisley is dead, don't believe a word of it. I'll be more alive than ever. I'll be jumping over the Hills of Glory. I'll tell you what I'll be doing. I'll be singing as I never sang before.

Brother Rod Bell put me off tonight, he is to blame! I want to tell you, when he gets to Heaven the both of us will sing a duet that will make angels fold their wings. I tell Willie McCrea I'm going to start my singing ministry in Heaven. He started his down below, I'm going to start in Heaven. The west window! The sun is going to set, and you know when the sun is setting it is a great thing to know that Jesus will never fail.

MY MOTHER'S SONG

My mother was a great Gospel singer. She had one favourite hymn, "Take your burden to the Lord and leave it there." I can hear her singing it now. I never knew who wrote that hymn until a week ago. It was an old coloured preacher who wrote that hymn. He was called Charles Albert Tindley. He was an old coloured preacher and a faithful man of God. He was to be elected to the Bishopric in the Methodist Episcopal Church many, many years ago, when that Church still had faithful Gospel preachers. That man had an enemy, another coloured preacher, and on the day that the vote was to be taken, in every seat of that Methodist Conference there was a letter addressed to every voting delegate. That letter accused Tindley of immoral conduct; lack of scholarly attainment and insensitivity towards his fellow ministers. It was a devastating attack that could not be answered during the voting period, and it resulted in the devastation of Tindley's chance ever to become a Bishop. He was completely and totally defeated, although everybody thought he would be elected. His shoulders sagged, his smile was replaced by a grimness reflecting his inner hurt. His character had been assassinated, his spirit crushed, and he was powerless to defend himself. For a short span Tindley could hardly bear the agony and the pain. It was difficult for him to immediately comprehend that his enemies, God's chosen servants, could have stooped so low. He had never known such pain and sorrow before. He went home to his little room and took up his pen and wrote that hymn:-

> If the world from you withhold
> Of its sliver and its gold,
> And you have to get along with meagre fare;
> Just remember in His Word how He feeds the little bird,
> Take your burden to the Lord and leave it there.

If your body suffer pain,
And your health you can't regain,
And your soul is almost sinking in despair,
Jesus knows the pain you feel,
He can save and He can heal,
Take your burden to the Lord and leave it there.

When your enemies assail
And your heart begins to fail,
Don't forget that God in heaven answers prayer,
He will make a way for you,
And will lead you safely through,
Take your burden to the Lord and leave it there.

When your youthful days are gone
And old age is creeping on
And your body bends beneath the weight of care,
He will never leave you then,
He'll go with you to the end,
Take your burden to the Lord and leave it there.

Leave it there,
leave it there,
Take your burden to the Lord and leave it there.
If you trust and never doubt.
He will surely bring you out,
Take your burden to the Lord
And leave it there.

IN THE EVENING TIME - LIGHT!

When the sun goes down, as it shall, upon my ministry, I'm not going to have any fear, I'm not going to have any problems, for I've taken my burden to the Lord, I've left it there.

Friend, I have one final message for you. Meet the Lord Jesus Christ. Just meet Him! Free Presbyterians can't save you. A preacher can't save you. A priest, prelate or pastor can't save you, but Jesus can save you. You just need to come to Him.

> Only trust Him,
> Only trust Him
> Only trust Him now,
> He will save you,
> Hallelujah!
> He will save you now.

And when the sands of time are running out for me there is going to be a blessed picture before me. A little boy of six kneeling beside his mother in the old church in Hill Street, Ballymena, where I knelt down and I found Jesus as my Saviour. That day started my pilgrimage for Heaven. It has been a zig-zag path. It has led me twice to jail. I don't know how many times I'll be back before I end the journey. It has led me into three parliaments. I think I'll have to go to the United Nations before I finish my course! I do not know, but this I know, that Jesus has never let me down and never will. People have let me down. I have let the Lord down. I say it with penitence of heart, and repentance of soul, but the Lord Jesus has never let me down. If I never see you again I want you to go home and remember that Jesus Christ, Ian Paisley's Saviour, was preached up tonight. I am preaching up the Lord Jesus Christ, lifting Him up.

Oh, sinner, come to Him tonight and be saved. Oh, backslider, return to Him tonight and be restored. Dear Christian friend, renew your vows and ask God to send upon Ulster an old-fashioned, Heaven-sent revival so that this land will be delivered from the wrath that is to come.

May it be so, for Jesus' Sake!

AMEN AND AMEN!

THE
❧ IAN R. K. PAISLEY LIBRARY ❧

OTHER BOOKS IN THIS SPECIAL SERIES

♦ **Christian Foundations**

♦ **An Exposition of the Epistle to the Romans**

♦ **The Garments of Christ**

♦ **Sermons on Special Occasions**

♦ **Expository Sermons**

♦ **A Text a Day keeps the Devil Away**

♦ **The Rent Veils at Calvary**

♦ **My Plea for the Old Sword**

♦ **Into the Next Millennium**

♦ **Sermons with Startling Titles**

❧ **AVAILABLE FROM** ❧

AMBASSADOR PRODUCTIONS, LTD.

Providence House
16 Hillview Avenue,
Belfast, BT5 6JR
Telephone: 01232 658462

Emerald House
1 Chick Springs Road, Suite 102
Greenville, South Carolina, 29609
Telephone: 1 800 209 8570